Endosements

"Innovation comes at the cross-section of diverse ideas, which is why it's so important to seek diversity in top talent with different skills, backgrounds, and life experiences. Hang's powerful story provides a guide to harnessing your unique edge to achieve your leadership potential."

*— **Rami Rahim,** CEO of Juniper Networks*

"The best business outcomes are achieved when teams bring diverse experiences and points of view like pieces of a jigsaw puzzle, where no piece is identical. Hang's book is a quintessential roadmap for immigrant women who are amplifying each other's unique perspective as they rise in leadership."

*— **Manjula Talreja,** Chief Customer Officer of PagerDuty, Board Member at City Year*

"There is no innovation if you are not open-minded. *Embrace Your Edge* highlights the importance of access and collaboration for all in the 21st century, in business and in our communities."

*— **Eric Yuan,** Founder and CEO of Zoom Communications*

"In a modern world of chaos, Hang opens her life journey to share the challenge of climbing the mountain alone. Her experiences open the mind to what we have to acknowledge if we really want to find success, peace, and fulfillment and help others along the journey."

— *Dr. Howard Dover, Director of Center for Professional Sales at The University of Texas at Dallas*

"Why feel like an outsider where you feel you don't belong anywhere when you can be an outlier and belong everywhere because of your unique perspective and value you can bring. *Embrace Your Edge* is just the guide you need to make it happen."

— *Mark Goulston, M.D. Author of Just Listen*

"Hang is a motivational force to be reckoned with. 'You win points by being bold,' and her book is exactly that. This much-needed message couldn't come at a more crucial day and age where we— surprisingly—still have more room to close the gap in gender equality."

— *Marjorie Morrison, Co-founder and CEO of Psych Hub, Author of The Inside Battle*

embrace your edge

Pave Your Own Path
as an Immigrant Woman
in the Workplace

Hang Thi Yen Black

Embrace Your Edge

www.hangwithhang.com

Pave Your Own Path as an Immigrant Woman in the Workplace

Copyright © 2021 by Hang Thi Yen Black

ISBN-13: 978-0-578-82799-5

Table of Contents

Dedication

---

to my parents for their bravery,
to my children who inspire me,
and to my ex-husband for his continued partnership

Foreword

If you aspire to climb the corporate ladder, it is important that you know that not all the steps are stable, some are hidden, and some may not even exist if you are a woman or a person of color. When the ladder was designed, the architect did not anticipate that people of different backgrounds, ethnicities, and origins would have the appetite, talent, and capability to climb the ladder and that many could scale it better than the original intended audience. If the ladder and the suite to which it leads were not intended for you, then you will have to use extra measures to get access to it. That extra measure, that "edge," is who you are—everything about you that makes you different and unique.

Every company that recruits on a college or graduate school campus sells the myth of meritocracy, "if you are smart, work hard, and keep your head down, you will go straight to the top of the organization." After working really hard, doing exactly what you are told, playing the game as it has been dictated to you, the truth begins to creep into your thoughts, eroding your positivity and filling you with doubt. It's not just about doing the 'job'–there's a lot more to this. The reality is that is NOT how it all works. There are other factors like, owning the power of your authenticity, relationship currency, sponsors, exercising your voice, asking for what you want, and having a personal agenda, that are essential ingredients to successfully scaling the corporate ladder.

When Hang Black, the author of this book, introduced me at a conference, I knew then that she had an incredible power. As a Vietnamese woman with a history of survival and resilience–she was discovering her voice, and with it, the power to create change.

Hang has written an incredibly poignant, deeply personal, powerfully relevant book for anyone that has ever discounted or failed to embrace the power of their unique identity and authenticity. As she reveals the intimate details of her journey from refugee to immigrant to a corporate success, she demands that each of us embraces every aspect of our journey–the pain, the loss, the victories, the successes–and unapologetically applies all of it as *the edge* that it is in order to excel. She challenges every company to recognize the deficits in a culture that smothers the opportunity and innovation available in the differences inherit in the women, immigrants and people of color who are there to contribute. It is a powerful, and instructive read.

– **Carla Harris,** *Author of Expect to Win and Strategize to Win,*
Vice Chairman and Managing Director at Morgan Stanley

Preface

My story is not unlike any other story of overcoming adversity. My story is not one of extraordinary accomplishments, but one of thriving beyond humble beginnings. I'm not writing it because I think I'm special. I'm writing it because I encounter so many talented souls who are worthy of notice and nurturing, and perhaps they will be inspired to conquer their world, as they choose to define it, with confidence and truth.

After a career of navigating in the dark, I share almost three decades of experience curating resources and developing resilience in hopes that women who have been unseen, and minorities who have been unheard, feel empowered to celebrate their unique identity. I wanted to deconstruct how the formulas for success won't work for them, because they weren't written for them. Without access to information, choice, or voice, the journey can be an unclear tangle of overwhelming obstacles facing immigrant women who wish to ascend to their own vision of success.

This book is written for those who did not inherit access, but who have clawed their way to earn every step forward. It is written for those with will and grit, who are searching for guidance to build their own powerful networks and to shape their own destinies.

This book is dedicated to those who are highly capable but may be exhausted or stuck.

This is also written for those in power who want to attract these scrappy ones, the often diverse talent pool who possess an innate entrepreneurial spirit. And for this audience, this book is written without anger or accusation, but with a simple mission to seek mutual understanding and support.

Chapter 1
Navigating in the Dark

*"A visionary is one who can find his way by moonlight
and see the dawn before the rest of the world."*

– Oscar Wilde

In the fall of 2019, I stepped on stage as a global sales leader representing a Fortune 500 company at Dreamforce, a contemporary high-tech conference with over 170,000 attendees and 16 million online viewers. It was a moment I could not have fathomed five short years before, when I was paralyzed from a decade of career stagnation. Filled with nerves but fired up to motivate, I closed my eyes to remember why I was doing this. Countless women and minorities who seek to be seen need more faces on stages that resemble their own. As the overhead audio called my name in the ominous "voice of God," I pulled my shoulders back to place one tiger-striped stiletto in front of the other. With each click of my heel, I emerged from the darkness into the spotlight to share my story of breaking free from the confines of generic formulas to become a scrappy woman, professional, mother, and leader armed with skill, will, and tenacity. I had arrived on my own merits, on my own terms with dignity and authenticity. Most importantly, I had survived the journey better, not bitter.

The Importance of Access

The circuitous road that got me to that stage was long and arduous, laden with unexpected obstacles for which I was ill-equipped. There's a lot of momentum around diversity and inclusion, but the conversation is incomplete without a discussion about access. Inclusion does not ensure equality. Without equal access to opportunity and resources, representation in the room does not ensure a voice at the table. Without equal access, valuable talent will continue to be left out and left behind.

Think about beginning a competition from the base of a mountain. It would be fair to assume that everyone begins their journey under the same conditions and equipped with the same tools. As some start ascending at different rates, you realize that some people have a jet to the top of the mountain, while others have a helicopter. Where did these flying machines come from, and how were you to know that they were even in play?

Different people have access to sherpas, tools, and gear that you may not have known you needed. Depending on how much access you lack, you may not even be aware that you are navigating *your* path in the *dark*. If you're born blind, how do you know that you can't see? How do you become aware that your world is vastly different from everyone else's? In the corporate world, one phone call from a connected parent or acquaintance, one golf game, or one cocktail after the right meeting can offer a significant advantage.

Those who grow up without access don't understand the concept, let alone how to get it or what to do with it. They don't know what they don't know. As immigrants, my parents didn't know about gifted and talented programs or the significance of the SATs for college admissions. The only advice they knew to give was to work hard and study hard. We weren't aware of preparatory materials, and we couldn't afford tutoring. As with most children of poverty, neither of my parents were college educated, and neither of their experiences provided lessons on navigating a political landscape at work. Grit, integrity, tenacity: these were lessons they could teach me in spades. But branding, networking, and executive presence were completely foreign concepts that I would have to learn on my own.

People without access learn to navigate in the dark with disadvantages others don't face. We buy into the myth of a complete meritocracy, because it actually does work for a while. We can get pretty far along with intelligence and diligence. But only to a point. Until it's no longer enough. Until networking and access matters. Until Ivy League university admissions favor legacy candidates. Until a competitive internship is filled by a parental connection before it's ever opened to the public. Until we're ready to ascend from the staff roles of doers to the line roles of leaders. Until external biases block our path and plant internal seeds of limiting beliefs that immobilize us.

It frustrates me when people nonchalantly throw around the phrase, "Don't be afraid to fail." It has its place, but that particular formula of success is not written for people for whom second chances are harder to come by and the ability to try again is a privilege. The rhetorical question, "What's the worst that can happen?" carries much more weight for people who may have only one chance to escape poverty or oppression.

There's more jeopardy in failing when resources are finite and access is limited. Wrecking a car may mean losing the transportation necessary to get to the job to make ends meet. Betting on an investment may require every last penny. If minorities without access go bankrupt, they can't go back to daddy for another million-dollar check. They can't go back to the bank to ask for another loan. If they blow an internship, they can't go back to mommy to ask for another connection. There are biases built into the system that made it hard enough the first time.

Failure is less of an option for us. And if we do fail, we have to learn quickly from the experience. Every experience is like jumping into the deep end of a pool without a float. In one of my favorite movies, *Gattaca*, a naturally conceived character explains to his genetically engineered younger brother how he won a race in open water after losing every time before.

Vincent Freeman said, "I never saved anything for the swim back." This is what it's like to compete without access against the privileged. I don't have room to fail. I have to work much harder just to be even, without the luxury of leaving reserves in the tank. So I'm tough on myself, I'm tough on my kids, I'm tough on my teams, and I don't apologize for any of it.

The advantage of adversity is having to learn to survive. This is the competitive edge that immigrants offer. They're tough, they're judicious risk takers, and they learn quickly from their mistakes.

The Leaky Pipeline of Diversity

According to McKinsey's 2020 study of Women in the Workplace, little progress had been made in diversifying the talent pipeline in the six years since they began publishing the data. Minorities and women continue to suffer from the "broken rung" in the career ladder, that critical first step to management. "Since men significantly outnumber women at the manager level, there are far fewer women to hire or promote to senior managers. And the number of women decreases at every subsequent level." The progression from individual contributor to C-suite increases for white men by almost 2x (35% to 66%). This comes at the cost of a drop off by one-third for white women (29% to 19%) and men of color (18% to 12%). It most significantly comes at the cost of an alarming drop off to only one-sixth of the original population of women of color (18% to 3%). Do we really believe the shape of these various pipelines is a direct correlation to a lack of ambition or capability in women and people of color? [see chart on next page.]

When our career plateaus at a certain level, we may run around in circles without recognizing that all paths lead to a dead end unless we find the hidden door and someone to give us the secret code. In the dark, we are unable to foresee pitfalls and we are unaware of shortcuts. We don't know how and where to look for ropes that have been thrown down to help us. We don't recognize or trust people who can help along the way.

We're also sometimes our own worst enemy. I've personally been too stubborn to accept help because I was *so* proud of my ability to do things the "hard way." I thought I was *that* good, when in actuality, I was only *that* arrogant.

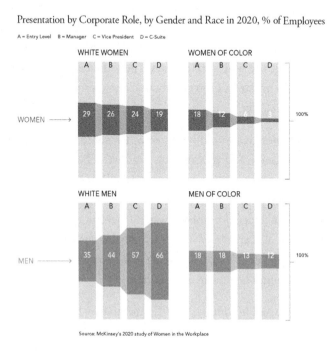

Presentation by Corporate Role, by Gender and Race in 2020, % of Employees

A = Entry Level   B = Manager   C = Vice President   D = C-Suite

Source: McKinsey's 2020 study of Women in the Workplace

My story began as a baby on an immigrant's journey that has defined me well into my adulthood as a person and a professional. I will share with you how actual war has prepared me for the internal war between the different parts of my world. In doing so, I will help you find the answers to some critical questions, such as: How do I find my identity when I'm the minority in the room? How do I rise in influence in the office when I'm expected to sit and submit, because it's what an outsider is expected to do? How do I find my voice when I've been taught to suppress who I am in order to conform to the predominant culture? And how do I comply with rules that keep changing around me?

As a child of war and grief, I understood very early on that change is constant, circumstances may be fleeting, but human resilience is immeasurable. Many immigrants share a similar story of displacement borne of necessity, but with very unique, deeply personal details and lessons. There are common themes of a flight from devastation and desperation answered by courage and resilience. Many escaped poverty, violence, or both. Many had to start over with nothing—in a new country with a new language, and in many ways, a new and conflicted identity in a new culture. In my story, I learned about clarity, resourcefulness, and the kindness of humanity.

These perspectives would be tested as I reached mid-career. Putting weight on diligence and meritocracy, I didn't believe much in luck or failure. Success was simply a product of intelligence and effort. Sound familiar? When my personal and professional world began crumbling around me, I concluded the problem was 100 percent my own. So, I worked even harder on my career and on myself, until I worked my way into the emergency room (ER). Twice. Realizing that destroying my health wasn't the answer, I sought help from every corner.

I felt like I had become a "true Californian" when I sought mental health. Apparently, it's a real thing. I invested time and money with fitness trainers and therapists. So, so much therapy, especially for someone who begrudgingly thought it was a hippy tool for the emotionally fragile. Great. Not only did I see myself as a complete failure as a mother, wife, and professional, I self-identified as "weak," a realization that didn't help much with the depression.

I sought professional advice from mentors and wisdom from books. They don't know it, but Carla Harris, Simon Sinek, Liz Wiseman, Malcolm Gladwell, and Tim Ferriss have walked alongside me in my journey for years. Yet amidst a plethora of insightful leadership resources and stories of adversity to prosperity, I still struggled to find a book that completely exposed the arduous and often undefined path for a perpetual misfit—

an invisible person who belonged to every community and none at the same time, someone with no access or blueprint, but who bore additional impediments of unconscious bias ingrained in my gender and skin.

I promised myself that if I ever overcame the obstacles in front of me to survive and thrive, I would share raw stories from the trenches, of an outsider figuring out her way, stories laced with harsh disappointments and learnings that would lead to triumphs over challenge.

Let's face the good, the bad, and the ugly up front. The good: you're intelligent, you're focused, and you're committed. The bad: the formulas for success out there won't work for you, because they weren't written for you. You will have to be more adaptable in finding more recently blazed paths. You might even have to blaze your own path and be your own hero. The ugly: life isn't fair. Your path on the same mountain may have additional obstacles than those of others around you. So just suck it up. Accept that it's going to be harder for you, then find the resources to help you transcend the additional barriers, because whining will only get you as far as the bottom of your next glass of wine. The good again (my positive nature won't let me end on a bad note): there are tools and people who can ease the ascent.

Access is about having all of the advantages of social acceptance and exposure to resources and support. This book is my way of throwing ropes down to lift you up. I will share learnings from piles of books and years of professional conferences, personal therapy, and executive coaching that may be out of reach for those who resemble a younger version of me. You will still have to find your way in the dark, but at least your tenacity will be complemented with better tools.

Finding Clarity in the Dark

Darkness has historically been associated with fear and evil. The saviors are the white knights and angels basked in white light, while the one who has been corrupted is the dark knight, or the one fallen from grace is the dark angel. Going into a "dark place" has been used to refer to experiences such as depression and addiction, while finding the light has expressed freedom or salvation.

I've never really understood the derogatory nature of the word. Why would you love the sun more and the moon less, when there is no reason to choose between them? I am both a morning person *and* a night owl. Each time of day brings forth a different mood and a different kind of productivity. For me, lightness brings energy and clarity while darkness brings mystery and creativity. In my life and career, operating in darkness has simply meant operating with more unknowns.

Those who always have enjoyed the full light of day may under-appreciate their complete line of sight to the top of the mountain, the shape of each trail, and a view of the pitfalls and shortcuts along the way. Having clumsily honed the ability to find my way in the dark without a roadmap or guide has become my competitive advantage. When the lights turn off leaving many disoriented, the scrappy ones are already prepared. When full visibility returns, those who have learned to be resourceful in the dark are better equipped to quickly assess where they want to go and how to get there. When change management is necessary, these tenacious survivors are agile, resourceful, and unafraid of change.

I can't define your endgame for you, and I definitely won't give you a Google map of the best route to your chosen destination, be it the summit or a vista along the way. Instead, I offer a trail map of routes, forks in the road, and pitfalls that I would have appreciated being aware of earlier in my career. I can offer a flashlight from my experience. Drawn from my own stories in conjunction with insights and brain science from thought leaders, I provide a framework of considerations to prioritize and decisions to make. I will share lessons I took too long to learn on terrain that was much more difficult than necessary. And if you find a path is closed for construction, you'll have the tools to reorient yourself to find another way to the top. This will be as far as I can take you. It will be up to you to take the first step with courage and to continue along your path with clarity.

If you have ever felt disoriented, diminished, or discouraged, I'm here to tell you that you are not alone. I *see* you because I *am* you. You've proven that you're not a victim and you're willing to do the work. You may have overcome socioeconomic disadvantages to excel in athletics, academics, and/or business. You may have worked your way through college, or you may have joined the workforce even earlier to contribute income for your family while you were in high school. You may have bravely started your own business with few resources beyond your own moxie. So, what next? How do you hit your stride, find your voice, and become your best self? I acknowledge the additional struggles you have faced without access and resources. I celebrate your bravery and encourage your continued determination. I assure you that someone *just like you* has faith that you can escape the narratives that other people have written for you. Where do you *want* to go? How do you *get* there? And what do you do once you *arrive*?

Don't fret. As Alessia Cara sings in *Scars to Your Beautiful*, "... there's a hope that's waiting for you in the dark."

Chapter 2
A Call to Undiscovered Heroes

"We must be willing to get rid of the life we've planned,
so as to have the life that is waiting for us."

- Joseph Campbell

When new employees ask my boss, Marcus Jewell, Chief Revenue Officer of Juniper Networks, for advice, he answers in a firm British accent, "Be clear, or get clear." I love the simplicity of this statement. My interpretation? *You* are accountable for shaping your own destiny. And yet, simple is hard. There is no one path because each road is as unique as you. It can be discouraging to follow formula after formula only to find they are all ineffective. The truth is that diet pills don't make you skinny and get-rich-quick schemes don't make you wealthy. It truly comes down to clarity, capability, and tenacity. The principle is *that* simple and the execution is *that* hard.

In one of the most viewed TEDx talks of 2009, *Start with Why*, and its corresponding book of the same title, Simon Sinek proposes that great organizations and leaders perform best when they are grounded in their sense of purpose, the "why." However, the physiological evolution of the human brain makes it difficult to find words to describe the reasons for our decisions.

The neocortex is responsible for all of our rational and analytical thought and language. The middle two sections make up our limbic brain, and our limbic brain is responsible for all of our feelings like trust and loyalty. It is also responsible for all human behavior, all decision making, and it has no capacity for language ... this is where gut decisions come from.

- Simon Sinek

That realization was mind blowing for me. Your decision-making center, your limbic brain, has no capability for language. This is why it's difficult to articulate the reason for a decision driven by the "why," whereas, we tend to communicate our decisions based on the tactics of the "what" or the "how" because these are connected to the neocortex, containing our language center.

If we can't explain the "why," there's a handy workaround. We can label the *values* that connect us deeply to our identity. The ability to connect decisions to core values keeps us inspired to be the best person we can be. It's hard to determine when to conform and when to rebel, but if you honor your authentic values, the right decision will inexplicably *feel* right.

In the Masters of Scale podcast featuring Marissa Mayer, a prior CEO of Yahoo, Reid Hoffman applauds her informed intuition. In the episode *How to Make the Star Employees You Need*, she shared her story of deciding to become employee number 20 at a teeny Silicon Valley startup called Google. Late on a Friday night in 1999, she was considering 14 job offers. Known for her vigilant reliance on data, she and a friend evaluated charts and graphs for 6 hours without resolution. Mayer made her decision after getting some sleep. "I woke up the next morning, and I just wanted to work at Google." She instinctively made her choice based on her values of intelligence and challenge.

How does this resonate with you? Have you ever needed more time to make an urgent decision? Did you go with your gut or did you deliberate? Reflecting back, if you had more time, what would you have done differently?

Shifting Your Mindset

I invite you to embark on a journey of discovery and transformation. Even when the destination is unknown, preparation for any voyage requires absolute clarity on the values that will ultimately define your direction. Before we begin, take a breath. Let me introduce you to a mindfulness technique that is important to revisit throughout your journey. I call it the three R's. *Reflect. Recalibrate. Reset.* Have you ever driven on a road and emerged out of a haze of distraction, only to find that you lost track of the last 20 minutes of time and have no idea how you've gotten to where you are? With your brain on autopilot, what have you missed: a turn, a short cut, or an interesting pit stop?

Several times in my life, I found myself running so hard that I didn't realize I was either already where I wanted to be, or I wasn't even going in the right direction. Stop. Listen to why, when, and where your heart beats. What does your intuition tell you? Release yourself from society's binary visions of male and female roles. Men are presumed to be either primary breadwinners or lazy couch potatoes. Women are either self-sacrificing primary caregivers or bitchy, barren, workaholic old maids à la the title character in the 2006 movie, *The Devil Wears Prada*. Imagine a world where you get to consider *all* the possibilities in between.

- *Reflect.* Get oriented. Take a really good look at your life and make an honest assessment. If you could wave a magic wand, what would your world look like? Is your life a complete shit-show from any point of view? Or is it actually quite good? Or the worst version: does your life look great on the outside, while you're withering in silence on the inside?

- *Recalibrate.* Are your expectations aligned to what the person you are today really wants, or are they an artifact from your history? What values do you want to take with you, and what do you need to adjust as you have grown?
- *Reset.* Self-awareness from the prior two steps is incredibly painful, but self-actualization from this last step is where the work lies. It is disruptive. It is uncomfortable. It is the responsible thing to do that will likely piss off people you care about, at least for a very difficult moment. This is the difference between dreaming or doing, between talking or acting. This is the choice between living on a superficial conveyor belt or stepping into courageous authenticity.

In the spring of 2000, my husband and I both had careers that were continuing on upward trajectories. The stock market was doing great, so we planned to do what all the other cool kids were doing and retire by the time each of us turned 40 years old. We planned to stay in Austin, Texas together forever doing heaven only knows what, with all of our projected free time. Our plans were driven by ego, without purpose. By 2002, we were expecting our first child while we were still recovering from the stock market dot com bust. We engaged a financial advisor who wisely instructed us to document a five-year plan. Learning from our earlier naivete, we decided to become way more financially conservative and (laughably) *reset* our target retirement to the age of 45.

Five years later, I sat down and opened my records to assess how we were doing against our goals.

- First child in the year 2002. *Check.*
- Save for a six-month cash contingency in case of another stock crash and/or job loss. *Check.*
- Second child in the year 2004. *Check.*
- Take kids on international trips to expand their minds. *Check.*

- Third child in 2006. *My brain came to a screeching halt. Wait what? The 2002 version of me planned to transition from a corporate to a philanthropic world, while my husband would move to a less-stressful government job. We were planning to be 70 by the age of 40. What the hell? Neither of us was anywhere near being done achieving in the corporate world. And we really wanted to continue funding our travel addiction.*

- Fourth child in 2008, complete with retirement for Hang to take care of the children. *Okay. This can't be right. Who was this person on the paper before me?*

Argh! The 27-year-old version of me thought I had it all figured out! Reviewing that document kept me accountable to my past decisions and decisions yet to be made. I had to **reflect** on the painful truth that personal growth had led me to become a misfit in my own world. I had to **recalibrate** as I started questioning why I was so proud of my motherhood, but incredibly ashamed of my ambition. That admission forced me to **reset.** I had to decide if I could find the courage to make the adjustments necessary to live authentically in the reality that life had taken me to, not the one I imagined. Otherwise, I had to decide if I was willing to silently suffer as I pretended that I had the power to bend reality back to the way it was before.

In evaluating your current reality, consider both external and internal factors. Adjusting to external factors, such as changes in the global economy, natural disasters, and unexpected personal life events, is tactical. Adjusting to internal factors prompted by personal growth in yourself, your partner, and other significant people in your life? That's a much bigger challenge. Are you ready?

Take the time to consider each of the questions in the next section thoughtfully. Grab your journal or take a walk and record your musings. It's easy to attend seminars and read books for thought-provoking inspiration, only to walk away and fail to self-provoke thoughts and action within yourself. In doing so, you miss the opportunity to actualize what you've just learned. It may be interesting to examine and review your thoughts a week from now, a month from now, a year or more from now.

Ask yourself, "What does success look like for me?" What is *your* personal definition, regardless of what has been prescribed by your parents, culture, environment, or even a much younger version of you? Work past your own biases and guilt by asking yourself what your goals are along the following three spectrums of success, or what I call the three S's.

- ***Significance:*** From *fulfillment to prestige*—what fills your emotional cup? In this moment, what is the balance you seek between finding internal gratification for the impact of your contribution versus the desire for external acknowledgement of your achievements by means of title, awards, and accolades?
- ***Security:*** From *basic needs to luxurious wealth*—what financial ability would make you comfortable? Are you seeking a certain dollar figure per year, and if so, what is driving that motivation? Are you looking to clear debt or take on additional debt to buy a certain-sized home in a specific location? Are you planning for an early retirement or aiming for obscene wealth that will afford extravagant vacations or even having a Learjet at your disposal?
- ***Stability:*** From *familiarity to adventure*—how much spontaneity do you need in your life? Excitement for one person creates anxiety in another. Tradition for one person creates boredom in another. Do you want to continue living in the community in which you were raised, perhaps with the support of your extended family? Or are you eager to move to another state or country to follow your next unexpected endeavor?

Internalize your first practice of the three R's by documenting your thoughts. ***Reflect*** on what you want out of your personal life and career by clearly defining where you want to land on each spectrum. ***Recalibrate*** your time. In this moment, what is the work-life balance you need to support the above? *Hint*: it *can* be, but does not *have* to be, 100 percent on either end. **Reset.** Structure your life accordingly. What changes do you need to make to actualize your new destiny?

The key is that there is no wrong answer as long as your self-assessment is current, authentic, and deeply personal. We are all instigators and victims of judgement. Practice self-compassion by disassociating from the guilt and shame of veering off the conventional road. This will allow you to realize your dreams. Otherwise, you may fall in the trap of adopting someone else's definition of happiness, jeopardizing your own definition to fulfill an external image.

The statement, "Resentment is like swallowing poison and expecting the other person to die," has been attributed to Nelson Mandela, St. Augustine, and even Buddha. My corollary is that "Fulfilling someone else's expectations is like watering your neighbor's garden and expecting yours to flourish."

Become Your Own Hero

Once you determine your purpose, you can become the hero of your own quest. Human evolution is dependent on our capacity to rise beyond the status quo, face challenges in unfamiliar territory, and emerge forever transformed. That's why stories from ancient to modern times follow a common pattern. In 1949, Joseph Campbell, a professor of literature at Sarah Lawrence College, created an archetypal hero based on his studies of myths from around the world. George Lucas consulted the author of *The Hero with a Thousand Faces* to craft the first Star Wars movie. The three acts of the hero's journey are summarized as follows:

- *Departure*: The Hero leaves the ordinary world as they answer a call to adventure.
- *Initiation*: The Hero is re-birthed into a champion through trials in an unknown territory.

- *Re-entry*: The Hero returns in triumph to share their secret formula.

Do you recognize the character development along these three stages in the origin story of each of the Avengers, the Last Airbender, or real-life hero, former Justice Ruth Bader Ginsburg? How does this resemble where *you* are on *your* journey?

1. *Reflect.* Have you accepted the challenge?
2. *Recalibrate.* If you are already in the trial, how are you going to conquer it?
3. *Reset.* What will you do once you claim the prize?

Are you actively listening for your calling? Have you ever felt a magnetic pull toward or push away from a situation or a person? And what are you going to do about it? Destiny has called upon you to delve into your fears. Let go of the reality that has been pre-defined for you, and bravely take the inner voyage to find your own fulfillment. In episode one of the 1988 Bill Moyers Interviews, Joseph Campbell indicates that we have to save ourselves in order to save the world. Fair warning: self-discovery will lead to a point of no-return. Catching a glimpse of your future badass self will be the siren's calling out of stagnation that you will not be able to unhear or unfollow. If you're ready to meet this better version of yourself, grab a pen, start an outline, and begin writing your story. Today. When I am resetting and starting a new chapter in my life, I hum along with Natasha Bedingfield, "Today is where your book begins, the rest is still *Unwritten.*"

Chapter 3
Courageous Choices
During Crisis

"The journey of a thousand miles begins with one step"

– Lao Tzu

At times, the path may seem unclear or the likeliness of success might seem insurmountable, but adversity hones resilience and resourcefulness. If my family could traverse 9,000 miles, or 14,000 kilometers, under dire conditions of war, we could survive anything. These early lessons provided me with a tenacity that would later be key to surviving the deaths of two parents, a lawsuit, a landslide, fleeing from wildfires, a home burglary, a divorce, six moves, and three layoffs. Life may push you down, but the strength is within you to get back up.

Envision Vietnam as a slender arm, from shoulder to fingertips, that hugs the southeastern corner of mainland Asia. This small southeast Asian country was dominated by China for almost a thousand years, then colonized by France for almost 70 years. Arguably the Singapore of its time, its people still longed for independence. In 1960, the Vietnam War began as a domestic mutiny and escalated into one of the most tragic wars among the superpowers in history, tearing the country and its people apart for 15 years.

Saigon fell on April 30, 1975, as my family watched from international waters while our country's capital was bombed and overtaken. My father, Mr. Hue Tran, was a major in the south Vietnamese army and my mother, Mrs. Huu Luu, was an elementary school principal. My parents were in their late 40s when they braved this journey with their five daughters and three sons that would set a course for the rest of our lives. In the span of weeks, they would make a series of impromptu, gut-wrenching decisions to risk our lives and leave everything behind—the family they grew up with, the modest property they had accumulated, and their belonging to a familiar community—in exchange for the chance at a better life.

Danang to Saigon: The Officer, the Angel, and the Cook

By the spring of 1975, it had become clear that Danang, the central city where we lived, just above the elbow, would soon fall into the hands of the communists. My parents knew we had to leave and make our way to

Saigon, near the wrist, to reunite with my grandparents and my two oldest sisters, who were living with them.

One evening a few weeks before the fall of Saigon, my parents took their remaining six children to the Navy port to catch a boat that would take us downstream. We joined people pushing and shoving to get to the end of the pier, but midway, my dad pulled our family back. He realized that in their desperation to flee, the crowds didn't notice that there were actually no boats on the other end. As the panicked multitudes pushed their way forward in the darkness toward the edge, the weight of the oblivious crowd only succeeded in forcing those ahead into the water, and to their deaths.

Appalled, but still determined, we sat on the uncomfortable ground overnight for boats that never came. As the sun came up, my dad left us to return to his post to avoid being court martialed for desertion. He was in command of a skeleton crew charged with burning military photos and records. Without my dad, and without a car, we would have to walk the miles home.

That's when the miracles started happening. A woman of quiet strength, my mother had an authenticity and kindness about her that was undeniably magnetic and would save our lives many times in the upcoming weeks. In the first incident, a kind-hearted sub-lieutenant spotted my disoriented mother with her six children in the street. With sympathy, he addressed her as "mother" and brought us to the Navy's headquarters.

Once inside, only few were guaranteed safe passage south. My mother looked beyond the rows of barbed wire laying on the ground between us and the Coast Guard boats getting loaded with families of Naval officers. Those smaller boats would take passengers to a ship anchored further away, destined for Saigon. Even with my father gone, she jumped on the opportunity for transportation, knowing that if both survived, my parents would find each other in Saigon.

My mother pushed forward to the front of the line until one of the men pointed his weapon at her chest and threatened to shoot her if she took one more step. We all squatted close to the ground. Encouraged by the officer who let her in, she whispered to us, "On the count of three, get up and run. We either live together or die together." And so, we did. 3-2-1. As my family ran, my brother, Duc 12, vividly remembers the sound of M16 rounds exploding by his ear. The soldiers shot *above* us, but they didn't have the heart to actually shoot *at* us. Each time we heard the guns fire, my family would stop, drop into a squat, look around for a visual assessment, and clear the next set of barbed wire. After a while, we would get up and run until the guns fired. Again, we would stop, drop, wait, and run again. It would take hours to cross less than a 100-meter distance to the dock.

At the dock, only families of officials were allowed onto the small boat; the rest were ordered off. Refusing to be removed, my mother instructed all of us to lock arms as the soldiers pressed the muzzles of their guns against the temples of her children. Speaking in a flat tone, one of the soldiers said, "We will start shooting at the count of three." My mother dared in response, "Go ahead." We closed our eyes in prayer. Guns fired, our hearts stopped, and our eyes flew open. The boat commander announced, "Congratulations, we will take you to Saigon."

From there, we boarded a tugboat that slowly made its way toward a much larger Navy ship, the Hải Quân 17. Once next to it, the method of transferring passengers from one boat to the other proved to be a challenge, due to the stark difference in sizes. Crew from the Navy ship would cast a single, thick docking line to connect the two vessels. Passengers on the tug waited until a wave came by to raise the smaller boat up by two to three stories closer to the deck of the HQ-17. One at a time, people would catch the line and then jump the two- to three-meter gap. Not everyone made it. Daunting for the adults, and even more so for the kids, the biggest challenge would be the toddler—me.

My oldest brother, 16-year-old Dat, had been carrying me, but he knew trying to jump while holding me would mean certain death for both of us. He intended to wait for the rest of the family to make the jump, after which, he planned to turn around and take me back home. At 16 years old, he was willing to accept separation from the rest of the family and sacrifice his own escape to take care of me on his own.

When it was my family's turn to make the terrifying leap, a complete stranger appeared next to us. Unusually big and tall for an Asian man, my brother describes this man with awe as a mighty angel, which I can't help but imagine with a full complement of divine light surrounding him. This angel then offered to throw the little one to the big boat.

As my mother watched with terror, she contemplated forfeiting the trip, thinking we would not all successfully make the jump. It was at that moment that my middle sister, Phuong, only 13 years old, leapt for the rope and made it safely aboard the ship. At her impetuous age, she determined the course of action for the rest of the family. We had to follow her. My mother turned to the giant stranger next to us and accepted his offer to throw me to another stranger above, who barely caught me by a single, chubby little hand. Miraculously, we all made it.

Once on the Navy ship, only families of senior officers were allowed in the interior. Locked out by metal doors, the rest of us sat on the slippery deck at the mercy of the wind and waves. Hours later, as an enemy ship approached, the Navy prepared to shoot a cannon, which would jeopardize everyone on deck. The sailors relented and allowed us to find our way into the belly of the ship. One of the cooks happened upon us and took pity on the seven of us in a tight huddle—nauseated, hungry, and dirty. He claimed my mother was his sister so he could bring us into the kitchen. There, he fed and sheltered us, the only family allowed other than staff, for the duration of the journey.

Saigon to Guam: Darkness in the South China Sea

By the time we made it to Saigon and reunited with my sisters and grandparents, the Viet Cong had invaded Danang. Over a week later, my dad was able to join us. As the northern army pressed southward toward Saigon, each military person's home was confiscated and re-issued to the communists. At one desperate point, my mother discussed preparing a final meal laced with poison in a suicide pact before the communists could find us. We all made our peace with the plan, if it came to that.

On April 29, our family of 10, plus two aging grandparents, vacated their house with the clothes on our backs, a small bag of belongings for each person, and two ounces of gold entrusted to my oldest brother. That would be the day before Saigon fell. My dad walked to the military compound and came back with two of his subordinates in a tiny white French sedan, about the size of a Volkswagen Beetle. Not knowing how long we would be driving around in such a cramped space, my dad asked a nearby family to let his parents, in their late 60s, stay with them for a while, with a promise to come back once we found safety. Unfortunately, this would be a promise we would break the very same day. In that car, we wedged two parents, eight children ages two through 17, and the two soldiers. If you're keeping count, that's 12 people ... and I repeat ... in a car the size of a VW bug.

Roads destroyed by cannon shells were blocked at every turn. We followed one detour after another, finding ourselves routed toward Bạch Đằng Harbor, where we discovered that a commercial ship, the Trường Xuân, was docked and ready to leave Saigon. My father knew this could be a golden opportunity that may never arise again. He also realized this meant we would have to leave his parents, who awaited our return upon finding shelter or an escape route out of the country. On the other hand, if we stayed, my parents knew we would be homeless at best, but more likely prisoners sent for re-education, or much worse. In a heartbreaking moment, my parents made the fateful decision to leave behind everything they had ever known.

Once we abandoned the car, the soldiers saluted my father to take their leave of us. As they walked away, they began peeling off their fatigues down to their underclothes to blend in with civilians. It was important to them to escort my father toward safety as far as they could, with the honor of the uniform. Only after they fulfilled their duty did they remove the very clothing that would clearly mark them as targets to the enemy. When I reflect on that story, I think of the type of leader my father must have been to inspire such love and deep respect by the people in his charge.

Many years later, in my late 20s, I attended my husband's grandmother's funeral in the small town of Swansboro, North Carolina. After the service, an older American gentleman sought me out and asked if I was the daughter of Major Hue Tran. Caught by surprise, I answered, "Yes, sir." And he responded, "Tell him this GI said it was an honor to serve with him on my tour." Apparently, my father made a cross-cultural impression, even during that divisive time.

At the port, there were no lines, just unorganized masses of people clamoring to get as far ahead as they could. People were pushing and shoving to get on the ship, crying and shouting amid the chaos. Our family was the last to board, and my middle brother, Phuc, 14 at the time, remembers being the last to jump onto the boat. With only one foot on the deck, a single flip-flop from the other foot fell into the water as the rope was cut. Once aboard, my two teenage sisters finally realized the implications of the day. They inconsolably insisted that we go back for my grandparents, sobbing, "How could you leave them? We need to go back. How could you?" verbalizing the internal guilt that already hung heavily upon my parents' hearts.

The commercial ship waited until the pitch darkness of night, when the Vietnamese fleet entered International waters. The Trường Xuân followed them out for protection. In the distance, the United States Navy's 7th fleet was waiting. Hoping the Americans would save us, our boat chased a frigate all day until the captain realized the warship was intentionally remaining aloof. We discovered later, they could only approach to provide medical rescue. However, the fleet would pick up people from floating ammunition barges scattered in the middle of the South China Sea. He docked near one that was mostly empty and unloaded his human cargo. Along with hundreds of others, we were packed like sardines on this barge, whose double metal walls were filled with sandbags. On that first night, we watched the sky light up as bombs fell over Saigon.

We were stranded on the barge for almost a week, as my family was part of the last of the mass evacuation. Like leaves floating on a pond in the fall, the waters around us slowly started filling with masses of small fishing boats whose residents were also trying to get onto the barges. The barges were already so full that we slept squatting or standing, leaving no room for anyone else. Vietnamese soldiers on the barge climbed the walls to shoot at the fishing boats, which returned fire. Some of the fishermen set their own boats ablaze as they attempted to leave their past behind. Flames quickly spread among the densely packed neighboring boats, and soon there was fire in the skies above and the waters all around us.

Looking over the side of the barge with some other boys, my brother recalls counting the number of black satin pants floating in the ocean. These traditional garments belonged to the drowning women and girls who were not as fortunate as us. My brother described in Vietnamese that, in that moment, "một mạng người không bằng một xu đỏ." A single life was not worth a single red cent.

There were no rations on the barges—no food or water. People relied on what they brought with them or scavenged leftovers from those who were evacuated before them. My sister remembers having to share her only pair of sandals, which were literally a hot commodity as protection against the scorching metal surface heated by the sun just above the equator. A family next to us offered my mother money for her food, to which she responded that paper money no longer held value. But in her big-hearted way, she said, "Let me tell you something, I will share our noodles with you, anyway. As long as my family survives, yours will too." And so, she shared what little we had. As hungry as we were, we needed water more than food. Only the two youngest, my sister Anh and I, were allowed to take sips of what little we could find. The rest of the family only got a few drops on their tongues now and then. If not for the intermittent sprinkle from the skies, my family would have surely perished of dehydration while we waited for rescue.

Occasionally, a frigate would dock next to a barge when they had humanitarian rationale to save those who were weak or dying. On that last day, my oldest sister fainted. When they finally came to get us, people climbed like ants onto the wall closest to the ship out of fear of being left behind. The wall collapsed backward under the extraordinary weight, killing them along with those behind them. The immense frigate extended narrow stairs at an angle down the side of the ship toward the barge. Survivors would have to step over the fallen wall, further crushing the bodies as blood seeped underneath.

Only women and children under the age of 16 were allowed to evacuate from the barge. Fortunately, my father learned English when he was sent to officer candidate school in Aberdeen, Michigan in 1955. In the military, a university degree is generally required to become an officer. In some cases, high-ranking enlisted service members may be recommended by their superiors to advance and transition to officers. Being sent to the United States for officer training was an honor he would remember for the rest of his life. And the English he learned would save our lives.

His language proficiency earned him a crucial role as a translator for the evacuation staff, and he was allowed to depart with us. However, at 16, my oldest brother was not permitted to leave. I can't imagine the torture my parents must have experienced, having one of their children torn away after abandoning their parents only a few days before. But onward they pressed and watched anxiously as each child braved the rocky waves to climb the steep stairs. Unable to bear losing another child, they held their breaths until we were all aboard safely.

Once on the ship, my youngest brother, Duc, collapsed. My father carried his malnourished and dehydrated body to a makeshift Red Cross tent to be fed intravenously. Being a commanding officer, especially in such a patriarchal society like Vietnam, my father was always very heavy handed. However, to this day, my brother warmly remembers that time, when my dad pulled each of his children onto his lap to feed them drops of water and when he carried my brother's limp body for care, as the most tender my dad would ever be to the boys in their lives, before and for decades after the war.

A little more than a week later, we docked at Subic Bay in the Philippines. Less than a day later, we were flown to the U.S. territory of Guam in the South Pacific. Unbeknownst to us, my oldest brother was picked up by the USS Nimitz a few hours after the rest of us, taken to Manila, and then also flown to Guam on a C-123. Operation New Life under President Gerald Ford processed almost 112,000 people who fled Vietnam in that mass exodus. At its peak, the tent cities housed over 50,000 refugees. Lonely and scared, my brother was wandering the streets when he randomly spotted my father. Dat had either lost or most likely had been pickpocketed of our gold on the barge. While it was clear at that moment that we really had nothing, zero, we were all immensely grateful that all ten of us managed to escape intact.

Although my mother's parents made it out with some of her siblings that year, it would be a few years before my father's parents and my parents were able to confirm each other's mutual survival. At first, refugees who arrived after us relayed sightings of my grandparents and other relatives in the old country, by word of mouth. Although we didn't really know what happened or where they were, we were just grateful to receive any communication about their well-being. We would eventually connect by telegram. It was still unsettling to wonder if the refugees were accurate or current, and if the telegrams truly came from them or an imposter seeking financial support from the United States.

Relief finally came when we received letters in their own handwriting. At first, the communications were cryptic as each side was justifiably paranoid about government screening of their private postal communications. This would ease over time. It would take 20 years for the United States and Vietnam to re-establish formal diplomatic relations. My father's parents never got out. They lived in Saigon the rest of their lives. My grandfather would never again see his only son or grandchildren before he passed in 1986. I recall my father sitting on his bed in shock as he held the telegram in his hand. I had never seen, and would never again see, him in tears as he whispered under his breath, "My daddy is gone."

After the political normalization, my oldest sister and her husband, my oldest brother, and my husband and I, were the first to return to our homeland to visit my grandmother in 1996. We were 17, 16, and 2 years old when we left. We were 38, 37, and 23 years old when we returned. Various grandchildren came back to visit each year, but my father was blacklisted by the Vietnamese government due to his years as chairman of the local Vietnamese resistance organization in Baton Rouge. He would finally be allowed to return to see his mother for the first and only time in 2003, two years before her death, and four years before he passed, as well.

From Guam, my family landed in Fort Chaffee, Arkansas, one of four major Vietnamese refugee processing centers in the United States. In less than six months, we would relocate to Illinois to meet our sponsor family, then we were off to Michigan to join my mother's siblings, before moving to Louisiana.

Settling in the Deep South

In Michigan, I distinctly remember snowbanks in the driveway taller than me and icicles thicker than my brothers' thighs clinging from the roof and touching the ground. My mother remembered my father's nightly tears, conflicted between gratitude for survival and exhaustion from the hard life we now found ourselves in. My dad didn't hesitate when a friend recruited him away from the bitter cold winter in Battle Creek. My parents had already made difficult decisions to disrupt their lives, what was one more?

My family set our roots in Baton Rouge, Louisiana, when Mr. Khieu Le, a former Vietnamese colonel who once guarded the 17th parallel (the provisional demarcation between north and south), invited my father to join him as a caseworker for the United States Catholic Charities (USCC). My father would work in this office with his friend until his retirement, intaking refugees who were fleeing crises from all corners of the globe, helping them get situated in their new lives. And so, it was that my entire childhood was filled with countless trips to the airport, greeting new arrivals fleeing global crises from southeast Asia, Ethiopia, Serbia, and other political hot spots. I watched the dedicated staff of the USCC help these refugees connect with their families, form communities, and provide access to a hopeful future until I left for university at the age of 17.

Following their trials, my parents created a new life of impact in the US and returned as heroes within their own community. Certainly, there are tragic outcomes as a result of unexpected situations, but there can also be clarity and opportunity for those who are courageous, resourceful, and tenacious enough to travel an uncharted path. From my family's journey, I learned that you must be deliberate in your goal while allowing room to adapt to a shifting reality.

How did they do it? How did my parents make impossible life-altering choices under immense time pressure and emotional stress? They were clear on their purpose, to keep our family alive. Based on their intuition, they decided to trust in the kindness of strangers, throw the baby onto a boat, abandon my grandparents and home, pile all of us into a tiny car, and escape our homeland into the unknown. These lessons on agile decision making would remain with me for the rest of my life.

My father's first job in the United States was as a janitor at a car dealership, and every one of my siblings over the age of 12 began working in corn fields or restaurant kitchens. As the last of eight children in a family where English was not the primary language and everyone was working to feed us, the only way I could contribute was to focus on my studies with a fierce commitment to earn their sacrifice. Although I don't have personal memories, I cobbled together the common thread of our plight among the collective memories of my parents and siblings. This history would guide me to become self-sufficient, and to begin contributing as early as possible. Because that's what immigrants do.

As the old adage goes, "The only thing constant is change." My life and career have taken unexpected twists and turns that would leave me disoriented and breathless. I have faced racism in school, sexism at work, and demons of my own making. Through it all, the best decisions I have ever made have been the most unforeseen, riskiest, and yet innately authentic. My worst decisions have been the most predictable, comfortable, and misaligned to my joy. The only way I could traverse the sands that kept shifting beneath me was to become deliberate in my goals, while allowing room to adapt to the everchanging reality around me.

Your Story, Your Journey

At the beginning of the last chapter, I asked you to think about what success looks like for you. Having survived the cancer that killed his father, Clayton Christensen reflects on how to live a life of purpose and integrity in his book, *How Will You Measure Your Life?* "If you're both calculating and flexible, you'll always find the right direction." Let your purpose be the North Star that drives your decision making.

We all have stories. The happy ones build our joy, and the painful ones build our strength. If you have been in pain, give yourself space to mourn it. Then leave the sadness from the chapters behind you and take only the lessons forth. They have made you who you are, but they don't have to dictate how you proceed on your journey in the chapters ahead. As Brandi Carlile unapologetically sings in *The Story*, "I climbed across the mountain tops, swam all across the ocean blue, I crossed all the lines and I broke all the rules." And you can too.

Chapter 4
Living in the "And" Culture

"I have put duality away. I have seen the two worlds are one."

– Rumi

Stereotypes exist because groups make judgements about other groups. Let's be real. We all do it. We form these stereotypes in silence when we're outnumbered, only to express our views when we're in the comfort of our own kind. My opinions are valued very differently when I'm sitting in a room full of white men, full of white women, full of minority men, or full of minority women. In fact, *I* am valued very differently depending on who else is in the room.

If we're going to be real, let's be *real* real. What is your definition of a minority? Is it race? Is it gender? Is it religion? Is it tenure? Even within the classic definitions, there is an unspoken social hierarchy based on the composition of characters. Who am I surrounded by? Do they have access to people and resources? Are they darker or lighter skinned than me? Are they male or female? Religious? Gay? Or both? It is heartbreaking to watch groups who bemoan injustices of discrimination turn around and do the *exact same* thing to another group they perceive to be "lesser" than them. It upsets me because it forces me to face the shame that I have committed this same sin many times before, myself.

33

It took me too long to realize that the weight of a single voice greatly depends on the authority and uniformity in the room. Who is already in a position of power, and who is the majority of the audience? In many cases, it's the same group. If one person in the minority somehow is accepted as an equal to the majority group, either by invitation or innovation, the fear of losing this precious access can lead to misbehavior. As an example, the Queen Bee syndrome occurs when high ranking women in male-dominated environments establish a hostile environment for other women. Historically, in a team of ten people in power, there may be only one token seat available to a woman. Therefore, another woman entering the field threatens the person already holding this singular seat. This lack of access to *all* seats triggers survival mode, creating a lose-lose scenario for progress.

The same is true with minorities vying for a token seat. The dirty truth is that after being discriminated against, minorities discriminate among each other. We don't talk about it, but we all know that favorability often follows an inexplicably unwarranted, but established pecking order that biases against women and darker complexions. In many non-Caucasian cultures, beauty is defined as a pasty ghostliness that is next to godliness. Therefore, the hierarchy generally looks like this: Asian men at the top, then Latino men, then Black or native men. This is followed by the same order for women: Asian, Latina, and lastly Black or native. There are situational variances where lighter-skinned women are regarded above darker-skinned men, there are judgements between races, and even among nationalities. I can't even begin to speak to other flavors of medium-tinted ethnicity and other social variables, such as religion, sexual orientation, or disability that are captured into a single category of "other."

The fact is it is lonely to be the only. A white man may be a minority in a room of engineers in the Bay Area. Intentionally or not, we make him feel just as out of place as he makes us feel any other time. No matter who you are, being the misfit in the room is uncomfortable. Being in a minority simply means you are part of the smaller group that's different. Full stop.

This is why representation matters. In a bowl of yellow Skittles, a blue one stands out. That's great for branding, but not for belonging. In a bowl of multi-colored candy, you are free to enjoy the deliciousness of each one. In a room of misfits, everyone's the same. Each person is more free to express their voice. Each can be seen for who they are and what they bring to the table as an individual, instead of being lumped into a group of "us" versus "them."

Inside the Outsider's Lens

As an outsider for the better part of my childhood, I was fortunate to live with dichotomies that were familiar friends who existed side by side in symbiotic peace. After the transition from refugee to immigrant, I grew up in the Deep South, smack in the middle of conflict between race, religion, and Eastern and Western values. I was an outsider, living in the void between black and white peers, between conflicting doctrines of a devout Catholic father and a devout Buddhist mother, and between an authoritarian Eastern culture and an autonomous Western philosophy.

People I loved held differing opinions, each equating their truth to *one* righteous path. It became clear that I would have to make my own decisions. Because I immigrated when I was only two years old, I was too Americanized for my ethnic peers. With my appearance and traditions, I was too ethnic for my American peers. I would have to reconcile the difference between my own experience against presumptions associated with what I learned from authorities about origin, gender, and archaic values. These lessons would teach me how to observe with curiosity and kindness, which has given me the perspective to engage in compassionate and impartial conversations.

My education began in Louisiana at Bernard Terrace Elementary School. I had male, female, black, and white teachers who I loved and respected dearly. I had friends of all types in a student population that was mostly black and white, with only a handful of Asian kids. It often surprises me when I hear people say, "My kids don't see color; they see people." I call bullshit. If you don't see color, you may not actually *see* the whole person. The difference is *choosing* whether to fear or embrace the whole package of the person standing in front of us by seeking to learn from each other's backgrounds.

Growing up through the 1980s in Louisiana, I was lucky to be assigned to a school that celebrated heritage, while acknowledging the flaws of a history of racial violence that bred current-day mistrust. With the state's rich cultural background, we learned about native Americans, the American Revolution, the migration of French Canadians to Louisiana, *and* the dark side of southern history that was central to the Civil War and the Civil Rights movement. Our Cajun heritage mandated French language lessons every week, which also opened a window into European history.

At home, I learned the Vietnamese language and Asian history. Wonderfully, all these cultures celebrated a passion for food and music. My schoolmates listened to Motown, pop, *and* zydeco. At home, I listened to Vietnamese folk music. I learned to square dance, electric slide, *and* ballroom. Even now, I choose to live in an "and" culture, unable to reconcile why anyone would choose to operate in a highly limiting "or" culture.

I didn't have to pick sides, I didn't want to, so I didn't. Up to that point, the most traumatic experience I had at school was the nervousness that caused me to add an extra "m" in "tomorrow," which cost me the spelling bee. I cried for hours. The struggle is real in grade school. I didn't realize how lucky I was to be in such a progressive environment. It's easy to under-appreciate it until you're removed from it.

For a few months in third grade, my mother and I moved in with her sister in El Paso, Texas, where my mom underwent treatment for cancer. I didn't know anyone, and worse, I was painfully shy and reserved, ripe for bullying. We lived too close for public transportation, and too far for a little kid to walk. I was one of the earliest to get dropped off and one of the latest to get picked up by my working aunts. I remember getting called "chink" every morning by the white and brown kids. In fact, I didn't even know what the word meant, having never been called that in Louisiana. From the tone, I just innately knew that it was demeaning.

I spent most of the mornings keeping my distance on the swings until it eventually got crowded and I would get physically shoved to the ground by some racist idiot. This happened almost every day. And after school ... ugh ... when the playground was vacated and the fences were locked, I would sit on the curb by myself, while boys biked by and sometimes spat on me as they passed. It was always the boys who openly harassed me. The girls merely shunned me—that is, until one afternoon when they decided it would be much more fun to beat me up. This was shocking. I didn't understand what was happening. It was not my experience up to that point. I grew up with kids of all colors, and no one treated me that way. I remember that afternoon very clearly. I remember the terror until the adrenaline kicked in as seven girls closed in on me.

The Japanese martial art of Aikido teaches the practitioner to redirect the opponent's attack momentum, essentially using their own strength and position against them. I had no martial arts training, but I watched enough Bruce Lee movies to get into a solid horse-stance that would ground my position. With a stubborn squat and two well-placed hands in bitch-slap-ready position, I simultaneously leaned into their stereotype of a slanty-eyed Kungfu kid and challenged their stereotype of a meek little Asian girl.

Now it was the aggressors who were disoriented and confused. Part of it was calling their bluff. The fact that I calmly prepared to take them on was enough to neutralize the mob mentality. Some of the girls shrugged and walked away. The others, well—let's just say I made it out just fine and I was never threatened again during my time there. It would be the first, but not the last, time that breaking out of other people's assumptions had a meaningful impact on the direction of my life.

I eventually made friends with some smart kids, some kind kids, and it turns out that some of these girls were among those groups, too. They were just misguided due to their own fears. I could have chosen to hate them, but wouldn't that make me just as bad? I don't believe kids are born mean. Ignorance and prejudice are learned mindsets, which can be overcome by kindness. I was misunderstood because I was misrepresented. The problem with stereotypes is the incomplete story it perpetuates by disregarding the individual human. Once these children got to know me, the threat was removed. My new friends learned that I was not the enemy. When they realized they didn't have to pick sides, they didn't want to, so they didn't. Even at seven years old, *they* were able to **reflect, recalibrate,** and **reset**. They could be cool *and* accept the new kid. It just shows that exposure to diversity brings the perspective that we are better together.

I often tear up when I tell this story, not because of any residual pain—that left me long ago. The memory hurts my heart to think of how many children must be in a similarly defenseless situation today, at the mercy of uninformed hatred. From an intellectual point of view, I can't even take this stupidity seriously from the sheer nature of its laziness. One would assume that if one is going to use a racial epithet, at least have the self-respect to learn the terminology.

Racial slurs often surface in wartime in order to protect the sanity of the soldiers by purposely dehumanizing the enemy. "Chink" is generally associated with people of Chinese descent; "gook" is generally associated with 20th century Korean and Japanese enemy soldiers. During the Vietnam War, communists were nicknamed "Charlie," a shortened version of "Victor Charlie," the radio code designation for the "Viet Cong." And if you can't tell us apart, you can generally call east Asians "yellow people," not to be confused with the cartoon family, the Simpsons. Get with it. Racism is uncool. Ignorant racism is straight up unflattering.

After my mother's recovery from surgery, we returned to my home elementary school in Baton Rouge. I am grateful for this out-of-state school detour that opened my eyes early to the unreasonable fear of misfits that can manifest as violence, even among children. It taught me to defeat the cowardice of bullying with the power of character. If I was misunderstood because I was misrepresented, I had to undo the damage by representing myself well. I approached my classmates with an open-mindedness they didn't afford me. I gained their confidence by offering friendship and help, while clearly articulating how my background shaped my perspectives.

Information is power. By offering my authenticity and being vulnerable enough to describe how I think, I shared *my* power. They reciprocated by sharing *their* power, in the form of acceptance and respect. In my career, I channel this inner seven-year-old all the time to "kill them with kindness and upper cut them with data." There is no strength in marginalizing a group you fear. Strength is the ability to adapt and turn an unfamiliar environment into an amenable one where everyone can thrive. It's the ability to Aikido the crap out of your barriers.

Access Begins Early

As immigrants, my parents were unaware of the gifted and talented (G&T) program that the school district offered. At the end of fifth grade, my teacher handed me an application and his written recommendation to attend a magnet middle school. Flattered but not confident, I declined. He attempted to persuade me again. I declined again. There were a few issues (excuses) in my mind.

- *I was practical.* Going to a magnet school meant I would need to find my own transportation. How the heck can a busy household with two working parents and five siblings, who went to college during the day and worked at night, transport me back and forth to middle school?
- *I was intimidated.* Attendance at a magnet school bypassed local districting, so kids had to qualify by testing in. I may have been a smart kid in a little pond, but how would I fare in a big pond full

of smart kids, whose parents were native English-speakers with resources to support their children?

- *I was traumatized.* A small part of me still suffered from that transition to El Paso where I was completely ostracized and physically threatened. I chose to follow my closest friends to our local public middle school. Safety in numbers with a familiar crew, right?

Looking back, I totally would have kicked that test's ass, and I totally would have rocked at that magnet school. The pain I wasn't brave enough to deal with at that moment only delayed my having to face the *exact* same issues when transferring into high school, and some form of the same issues repeatedly in my career. My teacher did everything he could for me. He brought forth the opportunity. He gave me an application, wrote a recommendation, and advised me as much as he could. The rest was up to me.

The fact that I didn't inquire more about the G&T program is on me. The fact that I was too lazy to figure out the logistics and too cowardly to take the leap of faith is on me. The fact that I never brought this to the attention of my parents is 100 percent on me. If you're thinking how harsh it is to put that much pressure on a nine-year-old child, you are absolutely right. That's the point. Children without access have to grow up and be responsible for our destinies much earlier. It sucks, it's unfair, but it's life.

The experience is different for each of us. Ultimately, it's having to fend for yourself in the simplest of ways. You may have parents who work late hours. You may only have one parent. If you're lucky, you're reheating dinner that your mom made for you in the morning. Otherwise, you're cooking dinner for your younger siblings. It's doing your homework alone with no one to turn to for help. It's filling out school forms on time by doing the work upfront for your parents, instructing them to "sign here," because you have to translate the documents. These days, it may be not having access to the Internet, a privilege that most people take for granted.

Just as I never told my parents about almost getting beaten up on the playground, I didn't have a conversation with my parents about middle school because I couldn't add to their burdens. That's what immigrants do. Or don't do. In fact, I don't think I started sharing these stories with anyone until I was well into my career. The necessity to take matters into my own hands would hone my tenacity and fervent independence.

As children with humble backgrounds, we have to consider basic needs, find our own academic support, and even be prepared to defend our own physical safety against schoolyard bullies. We have to create our own access by working harder to find opportunities that most of our parents' peers are already addressing on behalf of their children. We have to build community in a cohort amongst whom we are often the "only." It begins in childhood and continues through adulthood. People without exposure don't know the right questions to ask, and people without access don't know the right networks to tap into.

Nowadays, growing up without access isn't just about race. There are plenty of affluent minority families with resources and networks. Conversely, there are plenty of white families who come from humble beginnings who are excluded from access. This book is not written for my own first-generation children who now belong to the privileged class. These children have networked parents who justifiably keep each other "in the know" of the best programs and paths. These children may have one parent who can afford to stay home. Meanwhile, parents of children without access may be putting *themselves* through school while working multiple jobs to put food on the table.

Swallowed up by a much larger urban middle school, the division of classes and races quickly became clear. The few friends I followed from elementary school soon drifted apart. In contrast to my wholesome upbringing, I heard daily conversations on the bus about kids' alcoholic experiments and sexual experiences. It was not uncommon to hear of sixth and seventh grade girls getting pregnant, and the rumor of an afterschool rape in the gym was disturbingly unsurprising.

I found a new crew, or rather, they found me. It was my first experience having mostly Asian friends. Except for that short stint in Texas, I had always just belonged to a school community, so it was odd to belong to a classified group. I was always proud of my heritage, but having assimilated early, I was much too Americanized for my peers. Neither of us were wrong, just different. Individually, I didn't fit with my old crew or new crew. Not part of us—not part of we—I had to find the grace to just be me. Collectively, Asians were neither meaningfully included nor excluded. We existed and floated from class to class, our cultural teachings to be demure coming in handy when we were called upon to be invisible.

Clearly, my assumption that following the herd I knew into middle school would ensure my sense of inclusion was incorrect. The sands had shifted beneath me again. Running away from my fear of being an "only" ironically led me down a path that would guarantee it. The comfort I followed dissipated quickly. Over a frustrating three years, I thirsted for more academic challenge and less social challenge. Middle school would prove that race alone did not define community. I was a misfit on every level. It was time to find a community of shared values. I needed to be among "my people." It was time to locate the nerds.

Having learned from my earlier transition, when my eighth-grade teachers strongly suggested that I apply to a magnet high school, I jumped at the opportunity. I could find the courage to get out of my comfort zone by employing my yet-unnamed methodology for the first time. *Reflect. Recalibrate. Reset.*

Reflect. Most of the population of Baton Rouge High School came from McKinley Middle, the same school I was too scared to apply to in the first place. Dammit. I had missed a chance to create my network early. No matter, I could still start from where I was. My parents did not brave the muzzles of rifles for me to be afraid of changing schools. This time, I would be scrappy. This time, I would do the work to figure it out.

Recalibrate.

- *I was open.* I needed transportation. I could carpool, I would walk if I had to, I would figure it out.
- *I was confident.* What I didn't have in access, I would make up for in diligence and blow away the competition. I would figure it out.
- *I was brave.* If I could find a way to survive the mean girls of third grade and middle school, I could make new friends anywhere. I would figure it out.

Reset. Even between the ages of 9 and 12, I managed to learn a critical lesson, change my mindset, and adjust my behavior. Sometimes making a mistake provides the needed kick in the pants to avoid repeating it.

Baton Rouge High School (BRHS) was a culturally diverse school with a rigorous math and science curriculum that was wonderfully balanced with sports and arts. Acceptance into the magnet school put me back in my meritocratic melting pot, a nerd among nerds. Because of the caliber of education, admission was competitive. The class before me would produce Bobby Jindal, a future governor of Louisiana, and another student in my own year would be on the shortlist for Supreme Court justice. It was that kind of school.

Don't get me wrong, BRHS was not Disneyland. It had its own issues. In a valiant effort to ensure representation, the district required a 60:40 ratio of white to minority kids. As a result, in the first semester of freshman year, we had roll calls in homeroom every day. White. Show of hands. Black. Show of hands. Other. Show of hands. Although I had experienced being an outsider my whole life, this was the first time I was confronted with a label, "other." Not included. Not excluded. Inconsequential, except to function as a variable in a nameless equation. The intent of the roll call was not malicious, but the result was hurtful.

It may seem unfair to those who have had idyllic childhoods that there is now so much focus on adversity. But as a leader, I find that I'm especially inclined to hiring these scrappy ones. Their life experiences have taught them that there's a much slimmer margin for error, so they learn quickly. They adapt. They survive. And the best of them? They thrive with surprising energy and creativity during crises. And honestly, people who have survived adversity have already experienced their fair share of unfairness. So, yeah, maybe they deserve this break.

Access to a great high school education and academically ambitious peers is invaluable. Our teachers taught with high expectations that were matched by their own dedication. I would reference classics I read, grammatical rules I practiced, history lessons I learned, and calculus I practiced for decades to come. That education didn't only prepare me for university, it has also given me a broad foundation for conversing, writing, and problem solving with credibility. I credit this school for a curriculum that led to merit-based scholarships I earned from respected universities. Fun fact: Asians don't qualify for most minority scholarships. And even back then, the meager income of a social worker was too high for most finance-based scholarships. Without my scholarships and government financial aid, I would have been challenged to earn a college education. Access matters.

If you did not inherit access, tap into your tenacity to find or form it. In the upcoming chapters, we'll talk about claiming your voice, earning credibility, recognizing opportunities, taking risks, and paving your own way. It won't happen on its own. As a tenacious person without access, you have to *make* it happen.

> *"If it was meant to be, it will happen."*
> – said no scrappy person, ever

Belonging and Bias

As humans, and as children, we ache to belong. There is nothing more painful than the loneliness of onlyness. That's why religions practice shunning the disobedient, it's why prisons punish with solitary confinement, and why families disown their black sheep. Social rejection and isolation hurts. Not being acknowledged that you exist hurts. As an "other," invisibility is an unwanted superpower. If you already have to endure it, embrace the opportunity for observation and learning. Disassociation from any group gives the ability to combat confirmation bias that one group is superior or inferior to another. Distance provides an objective view of both good qualities and fallacies of all people. Learn from textbooks and authorities. Then unlearn with compassion from your own experiences. I no longer worry about fitting into a group. Now, I focus on belonging to myself. This gives me the freedom to subscribe to a community of my own choosing.

And who comprises this group of which I speak? How do I identify them? Put simply, we bring out the best in each other. We inspire each other with endless possibilities of "and." We're not limiting each other to binary choices of "or." We are generous in sharing access to our expertise, resources, and networks. In the company of my community, time accelerates. We connect on an intellectual and emotional level. They're uplifting, not diminishing. I'm engaged, not frustrated. We're conversing, not pontificating. There is a mutual respect that draws us together by choice, not by obligation or similarity.

I invite you to think about your relationship to inclusion and access. This is just between you, your thoughts, and your journal. So, let's get *real* real on the biases you face and the biases you make.

Reflect. What are three groups you most identify with, and in which order (generation, gender, race, religion, socioeconomic status, sexuality, etc.)? What are three adjectives you would use for each? Are these characteristics positive or negative? What groups do you least identify with, and what are their attributes?

Recalibrate. What is the information you used to base your assessment of the groups to which you belong and the groups to which you don't belong? How much of the information was learned anecdotally versus experienced directly? Think about limiting beliefs you may have of your own group or other groups.

Reset. What negative correlations can you let go of to make room for what each group may have to offer? Are any of these limiting beliefs impacting your clarity? Are any of these limiting beliefs closing the doors to access in front of you? Make a plan to consistently tap into your strengths to find or form your own access. Think about expanding your community. How can you bring missing Skittles into your candy dish?

Our differences and our flaws are what makes us collectively complete. We don't have to be afraid of the others. Inclusion provides opportunity to hear different perspectives that are uniquely shaped by diverse experiences. Inclusion ensures that no one is left out. Access ensures that no one is left behind. I challenge individuals to accept their gift of adversity. The disorientation of immigration, the disadvantage of poverty, the frustration of being excluded can spark a priceless hunger. That drive is a competitive edge for you. I challenge organizations to embrace the relentless tenacity of these scrappy professionals. That drive is a competitive edge for your company.

Channel the ensemble from the Greatest Showman, "I'm not scared to be seen, I make no apologies, *This is Me.*"

Chapter 5
Sit Down and Shut Up

"Fight for the things that you care about, but do it in a way that will lead others to join you."
– The Notorious RBG, Ruth Bader Ginsburg

I've always been a high performer. When I've succeeded in my career, my managers appreciated the productivity of a high achiever. At other times, the halo of my performance was tarnished by judgements about my potential or ambition. When I have not succeeded, I've pretty much been told to sit down and shut up. Tempering my voice, I became inauthentic, less creative, less productive, and my performance suffered, initiating a downward cycle into the abyss where careers go to die. While I internalized ambition as simply a desire for achievement, the outward perception was filled with complicated judgements around my motivation. Ambition is a characteristic that is appreciated and even expected of men. Ambition in a woman of my generation is often met with a confused disdain and suspicion, as if broccoli-flavored ice cream was offered for dessert.

Every aspect of my place in life demanded suppression of my voice out of respect for traditional views of gender, birth order, religion, and established cultural norms. There are many ways to tell someone to sit down and shut up, and I'm pretty sure I've heard most versions of most reasons. As the youngest of eight children in a poor, non-native English-speaking family, and a petite female raised in the Deep South to boot, heaven forbid if I had a contradictory opinion to, well, literally anyone. That would be wholly subversive (insert eyeroll here). My designated place was pretty low on the totem pole of access and authority. Growing up without choice or voice, it has been that much more important for me to find mine and amplify others.

While acknowledging the pain and suffering of the horrendous Vietnam War, there is a silver lining in the many lives saved. As a female product of a very patriarchal culture, my choices would have been much more limited had I been raised in my motherland. The limited voice my sisters and I have had would be swiftly stripped away as soon as we got married. In a culture where marital unhappiness was an acceptable price to uphold traditional societal norms, rampant domestic violence was tolerated. From a remarkably selfish perspective, I'm very grateful for the opportunities that our immigration to America has provided for my family, and I'm sure for many others.

Immigrant parents struggle with how much to allow their children to assimilate into American culture, while honoring their own heritage. As children grow into adults, they have to define for themselves who they want to be, between their parents' traditional expectations and the person America allows them to become. As acculturation occurs, minorities incorporate themselves into the majority culture either by choice or trauma, by adapting to and even adopting the values of the prevailing environment. In doing so, the struggle is holding onto their unique identity. My dad encouraged me to only speak English at home to accelerate my assimilation, while my light-skinned friends of other ethnicities were encouraged to pass as white.

Deviation from traditional norms can cause immense friction within families and communities. Proponents of the differing culture feel betrayed and left behind, while the next generation is torn between the promise of belonging in the prevalent culture or the shame of disappointing their community. I was stuck between Eastern deference for social hierarchy and Western reverence for individualism. My Eastern background demanded that I abide by anyone older, but not necessarily wiser. Let's call this "ordained authority." Above and beyond the automatic gravitas offered by age, there was the general acceptance of male superiority. When describing a neighboring family's dynamic, my parents had a hard time explaining to an Americanized toddler why the opinion of a fifth-born son carried much more weight than those of his four older sisters.

Fortunately, no matter the school or environment, every last one of my teachers in Louisiana was color blind, gender neutral, and birth-order indifferent when it came to nurturing my potential. They encouraged my curiosity, built my confidence, and challenged me for more than I knew was in the realm of my capability. I was lucky to have these influences to validate my voice and to escape the narratives of my upbringing. Educators have a lasting impact on young minds to either empower or diminish, and there is plenty of documentation of hidden biases beginning in primary school that extend into university.

In my first year at the University of Texas, I had a professor who taught from a chemical engineering textbook that he authored. He offered to pay any student one dollar for each unique mistake we found. It was the first example I saw of awareness to recognize that each of us is only human and a brilliant way to crowdsource improvement. Our professor leveraged the sharp eyes of junior talent to review ground he had covered so many times that he lost the ability to see. I quietly stored this lesson into my toolkit.

In contrast to this empowerment, a childhood friend recalled a sign in one of her classrooms that read, "There are two rules in this class:
- Rule #1 The teacher is always right.
- Rule #2 When the teacher is wrong, refer to rule number one."

My young mind had no words to express the instinctive revulsion that my adult mind can now articulate as, "W. T. Actual. F?" Is your brain able to process those statements? Because mine can't. I don't think it's even meant to make sense. I think it's meant to be cute. News flash. Not cute. The philosophy of "the teacher is always right" introduces children to a world where their curiosity is squashed, and their opinions are diminished. Without being allowed to question, being right doesn't matter. Sit down and shut up. Follow the rules, keep your head down, and just be grateful to be here.

As children, we're blessed with the gift of wonder. How many times have you heard young children ask, "Why?" When my children were in grade school, I used to jokingly comment that I needed to get a Fitbit for my daughter's mouth so I could regulate her to 10,000 words a day. At the end of especially taxing workdays, I would instruct them not to ask me questions for a while—Mommy had decision exhaustion. To which they would promptly respond, "For how long?" Most of the time I was exasperated, but sometimes I would break out laughing in awe of the incessant inquisitiveness of their expanding minds.

It still makes me hyperventilate a little to read this paired principle. It's the equivalent of "because I told you so," which is already irritating as a child, but as a grown-ass adult? If you don't think adults hear this, let me rephrase in more familiar language.

Microaggressions:
- Are you lost? This is the engineering building; HR and marketing are across the street.
- How can you take a job away from a man who needs to support his family?
- Can you take notes during the meeting since you have the best handwriting?

Genuine lack of awareness:
- How does it feel to get a job just because you're a ____ *woman, minority, poor or any other disenfranchised group*?
- What barriers? What glass ceiling?

Assuming a lack of understanding:
- This is how things have always been.
- When you're more experienced, you'll understand.
- It's too complicated for me to explain to you.

The "momsplain" (my own addition!):
- You have the privilege of motherhood; why do you feel the need to be ambitious?
- How will you be able to raise your family while meeting the demands of a career?
- Surely you don't want a project that will require the hours or travel?

And drumroll ... The "mansplain" (my favorite!):
- Well actually, ... (Proceed to repeat exactly what just came out of my mouth but with authoritative arm waving and self-gloating at the end of how brilliant you were.)

If you are a young woman or the parent of a young girl shaking your head at the absurdity, let me assure you that these are my firsthand experiences, not secondhand anecdotes. Some of these statements were even accompanied with a literal pat on the head in a "there-there" motion. If you're astonished, don't be. I can feel some of my professional sisters out there nodding their heads in shared sympathy. Unconscious bias is real. There is a myriad of subtle and non-subtle ways to demand submission and compliance to the status quo. The first step is recognizing if you've been asked to give up your choice or accept a choice you never even made. You can recognize when it doesn't *feel* right because it won't *sound* right. Let's break down the dynamic of the above statements before we uncover some appropriate responses.

Let's Just Be Adults

In one of my executive coaching sessions, I learned of a psychological theory called Transactional Analysis, which was developed in the 1960s by Eric Berne M.D, author of *Games People Play*. This concept breaks down the components of human interactions, which consist of a stimulus and a corresponding response. The framework identifies three ego states: Parent, Adult, Child. The Parent and Child ego states are each a collection of recordings in the brain of a child up to the age of approximately five years old.

- The **Parent** state is how a child records *external* events as *lessons* or *teachings*.
- The **Child** state is how a child stores the *internal* response to events as *emotions* or *feelings*.
- As the child learns to evaluate data, they develop an **Adult** state that is objective and analytical. Berne describes the Adult as being "principally concerned with transforming stimuli into pieces of information, and processing and filing that information on the basis of previous experience."

The Parent and Child ego states are further subdivided as follows:
- A Parent is either controlling or nurturing.
- A Child is either compliant or rebellious.

These different ego states exist in all of us in different proportions, unique to each of our personalities. A *complementary* transaction is when a stimulus extracts an *expected* response, whereas in a *crossed* transaction, the response is *unexpected* and can be received as offensive.

When I first learned of this, it explained so clearly what I had been experiencing during my entire career, until recently. Right or wrong, something in me had been triggering the Parent or the Child in others, and vice versa. In a male-female dynamic, it's often the case that the woman gets diminished, or treated like a child that needs to be admonished or taken care of. Let's look at how society frames us.

In his book, *Men are from Mars, Women are from Venus*, Dr. John Gray explains that women like to counsel each other, while men hate receiving advice unless they ask for it. Another newsflash. Women hate unsolicited advice, too. However, the narrative is that arguments occur when a woman wants to "vent" about her problems, and she gets upset when a man jumps in to fix her problem. How is this NOT the same as a man reacting poorly to unwelcome advice on how to fix his issues?

At home, she is reacting to the emerging Parent, when all she needs is her Adult partner. At home, the Adult response can actually include just listening. At work, we need to problem-solve, and she's aware of that. In that coaching session, I realized that the rebellious Child in me gets activated when somebody gets all grandpa on me and gives me advice I'm not seeking. I am inviting you to ideate *with* me, not *for* me. Women may be more willing to be vulnerable in asking for advice more often, but that doesn't mean it's open season for unsolicited pontification. Asking for advice doesn't make them weak; it makes them curious.

Since we're all adults in the business world, let's act like it. In superior-subordinate relationships, **Parent-Child** complementary transactions can absolutely occur in the form of guidance and feedback. Outside of that dynamic, seek to keep conversations in the **Adult-Adult** model. It is the most efficient and effective form of communication, where problems are solved, and each person feels that progress was made. In the Adult state, we're doing things and thinking in ways that help us to be effective. We're objective. We talk about facts, we gather data, we analyze. If we have an emotional reaction, we communicate it without judgement.

Although business conversations typically begin well, friction can occur when the transactions get crossed and someone takes offense. Whether intentional or not, if one party is perceived as taking on a Parent state either by criticizing or smothering, it may trigger the recipient's rebellious or compliant Child state. Conversely, if the initiator of the transaction takes on a helpless, martyrish Child state, it may trigger the recipient to become the Parent in the room. In either case, the conversation deteriorates into an inappropriate **Parent-Child** dynamic from analytical problem solving into futility.

Let's carry this into the office with some business examples.

In response to an Adult stimulus: "The report is due on Friday."
These Child state responses result in a *crossed* transaction:
- *Rebellious*: Your deadlines are always unreasonable.
- *Compliant*: I will move everything around to meet this deadline.

This Adult response results in a *complementary* transaction:
- Here are some challenges I might have, and tradeoffs I need to make to meet this deadline.

Can you hear the difference?

Another Adult-Adult complementary transaction:
- *Question*: Do you prefer option A, B, or C?
- *Answer*: Based on the data and my experience, I recommend option B.

If you feel the conversation slipping, take ownership of your part in the dance. In the Adult ego state, we're making decisions in the moment, based on fact, without bias or assumptions, and communicating in accepting language. As a Parent in the office, we could be either too critical or too nurturing. We're either looking after people too much or setting rules outside of our domain. As a Child in the workplace, we could be too compliant, or we could be too rebellious and do things we shouldn't be doing. In either case, get back to the Adult state by using the three R's to redirect the conversation.

Reflect. Analyze your interactions. If you are feeling belittled, observe when *you* stray from an Adult state into a compliant or rebellious Child state. What triggered *your* reaction? What did it *sound* like? What words were used? What is *your* ownership? Did you exhibit childlike behavior to trigger a well-meaning Parent in your peer? Did you prematurely take offense?

Majority in the Room: STOP being overprotective. Your colleagues may repeatedly celebrate the anniversary of their 22nd birthdays, but trust me, they have long since passed the age of 18. They are self-sufficient and fully capable of making their own choices and managing their own workloads. Take a look around the room. Are you in the majority? Note that the more there are of the same people, the more of a voice that group has. Notice the minorities in the room and offer them the space to share *their* voice.

Minority in the Room: STOP suffering quietly. Raise your hand when you want to take on more responsibility, rather than hoping it will be given to you. Articulate when you are overloaded and need support, especially if you feel like you may have a disproportionate share of the "office housework," such as note taking, meeting making, or party planning.

Establish trust with each other that, as adults, we will raise our hands when we have the ability to and we will ask for support when we need it. No one is a victim here.

Recalibrate. Regardless of whether it was warranted, modify *your* behavior to bring *yourself* back to the Adult state, giving your fellow conversationalist the opportunity to realign their state, as well.

From my background of being an outsider with perspective from all cultures, and with my exposure to inherent biases from my own communities that truly wanted the best for me, I respect the origin of another person's beliefs. Everyone has a story that shapes their way of thinking. It took years for the control freak in me to accept that no one has control over another person's history, thoughts, or actions. I only had control of *my* own thoughts and reactions.

Reset. The challenge is to deliver an argument respectfully, in a way that can be heard by the audience to bring both people back to the Adult state. Aikido yourself out of a souring conversation by:

- having the grace to consider the other person's point of view and their belief system
- invoking the power of authenticity to invite the other person's vulnerability
- arming yourself with information and data to bring objectivity back into the conversation
- mastering the art of good questioning to provoke introspection
- having the confidence to pull yourself or your conversational partner out of the Parent or Child state

Corporate environments reward knowing the answer, which in turn, rewards the behavior of insistence on being the smartest person in the room. But what if we took a lesson from academia and stepped back to consider if we're even asking the right questions? Let's assume for a moment that the person who is making you feel like a child is not a close-minded, misogynistic, racist ass.

- What questions can you ask with genuine curiosity that could help them embrace your idea?
- What data can you present to neutralize an emotional argument?
- Discuss confirmation bias, theirs *and* your own.
- What story or part of yourself can you be vulnerable enough to share?
- What mutual value can you discuss to draw you both back to a mutually respectful Adult state?

Let's bring together a few concepts of questioning "ordained authority" that will keep the conversation in an Adult-Adult model.

The College Career Center

During my senior year in the College of Engineering at the University of Texas in Austin, we were given a set number of points to "bid" on job interviews. The first week, I bid conservatively based upon the confidence in my GPA and three semesters of intern/co-op experience during my last two years. Nada. The second week, I bet big on a few companies where I really wanted to interview. Nada. By the third week, I bid all of my points and was extremely frustrated when my name didn't appear in even one of the dot matrix printouts taped to the windows of the career center. Instead, I recognized the same student names week after week, when I knew I had a much more competitive background.

I went into the career center and had a conversation with a counselor:

Me: "Do you send resumes to the recruiters in alphabetical order by last name?"
Counselor: "As a matter of fact, we do. Why do you ask?"

Me: "Do you think that practice might bias toward those in the earlier part of the pile?"
Counselor: "Absolutely not."

Me: "If I'm a recruiter looking for 20 candidates, and I find them within the first 100 of 500 resumes, I would be tempted to stop. Have you thought about randomizing the resumes when they go out?"
Counselor: "That would never happen. We give them clear instructions to review the whole pile fairly."

Me: "I don't think it would be intentional, but I'm sure it happens."
Counselor: "We've been doing this for years. I can assure you that's not what happens. Honey, I'm sorry, you must not be getting any interviews."

Me: "Would you come look at the postings on the windows with me."
The counselor begrudgingly follows me out.

Me: "Of all these sheets, you'll notice that every single selected candidate has a last name beginning in 'A through M.' Not a single candidate's last name starts with 'N or after.' I'm sure if you check last week's, and the week before, you may find the same. My last name is Tran, and I'd really appreciate any help you can offer to make the system more fair."
Counselor: "Odd."

The engineering career center changed its policy the week immediately after, and I started getting my fair share of interviews.

In this example, I questioned someone with authority, without presuming malintent. When they started becoming defensive and taking the Parent state of "You wouldn't understand," I continued to reveal my thought process, respectfully. When they started being a little condescending, I continued to press factually. When I got their attention with the data, I provided an opportunity for them to not only bring fairness to a system in general, but I personalized that value to one person, me. This short, respectful interaction influenced an established institution's process, and I'm thankful for their willingness to listen and adapt.

I could have chosen to give up and sit out. "Woe is me. Why isn't my name on those interview sheets?" I chose to analyze the situation without judgement and inadvertently found something that was intrinsically wrong in the system. It was not intentional. But it was missed by those who had lived the process every day. It took an outsider to shed light on a problem that the insider couldn't see.

In action and communication, listen and speak with authenticity and without judgement. We take on these roles in different moments when dealing with different people. Think about when you mimic each of these states. How did you behave, what did you think, what were you feeling? And how do you react to certain people and circumstances? By engaging thoughtfully, you can shift the conversation from "ordained authority" to what I call "organic authority," which is earned by experience and expertise. If you can keep your emotions under control, you may be able to change something bigger than yourself, regardless if you're a seasoned old fogie, a fresh new intern, or even a 20-year-old college senior.

The Impasse

In a work example, one of my job roles along the way was to forecast revenue for a high-end routing business unit. Before Salesforce became prevalent, I got pretty good at wielding my Excel magic with complex formulas and mad pivot tables. As a result, I was asked to expand my role across multiple product lines. The manager who ran it previously was really upset that I was bringing in a new methodology, and he escalated the issue to our director.

Director: "Why are we here today?"
Other Manager: "Hang is significantly changing how we calculate the forecast."
Me: "My process is simpler."

Other Manager: "Your process is too simple."
Me: "Simple is hard."

Director: "Hang, what is motivating your change?"
Me: "I was asked to bring in best practices from my experience, which will save us time and improve results."

Director to the Other Manager: "Have we given Hang's method a try yet?"
Other Manager: "This would be the first month, but this is not the way we forecast in this business unit."
Me: "With all due respect, this business has not met the corporate target for accuracy of 90%. I was brought in because of my record of consistently beating the target on a $1.1 billion portfolio."

Director: "Hang, what is preventing you from running the more complex method?"

Me: "I could, but it will take me three times longer, meaning you'll get results weeks later, that I'm quite sure will be less accurate. I'd like to ask both of you for your trust. If in two cycles we don't see an improvement, we can either go back to the previous method, or I'll work with you to craft a better system."

Director: "This feels like a no-brainer."

This issue was never brought up again. Inside, I was fuming. I really resented getting called out in front of my director, forcing him to act as a Parent mediating between two children. This person wasn't even my manager, but he adopted a Parent stance that triggered my petulant Child. "No! You can't make me!" My initial language was exasperated and curt. Although within his right as our leader, my director chose *not* to be the Parent. His line of questioning brought me back into an Adult state, where I kept firmly to the facts of why I was brought in and what I had to offer. I became calmer throughout the rest of the conversation as I laid out my case. I uncoupled emotional attachment to a method by focusing on the data behind past success. And I ended with a reasonable ask and a willingness to pivot.

Diminishers

As always, it takes two to tango. If you believe you've done everything you can to be the adult in the room, and you continue to struggle with certain people or circumstances, then consider if you are in a situation to succeed. You may just be working with a "diminisher." In *Multipliers, How the Best Leaders Make Everyone Smarter*, Liz Wiseman describes a "multiplier" as someone who inspires you to be your best and makes you feel like you were born to do your job. In contrast, a diminisher stifles ideas by demanding recognition of their own intelligence, rather than taking advantage of the potential in the team. They make you dread going to work. According to Wiseman, the five strategies that don't work with diminishers are confrontation, avoidance, quitting, lying low, and ignoring. Instead, she makes the following recommendations:

1. Defuse the conflict by making a suggestion that combines both of your ideas.
2. Remind the person of the specific expertise for which you were brought into the team.
3. Use their skills to your advantage by proactively bringing them into the discussion and asking for their key insights at the time of your choosing. Invite them, rather than shutting them out, so they can see your talent firsthand. Engage them at specific moments of your choosing, while you take the lead in driving the initiative.

Diminishers suffer from generosity deficit disorder. They want control and attention. Counter this by being generous with your attention, without relinquishing your control. It is important to remind them of the skill set that you bring to the table. Acknowledge their expertise and remind them of areas where you agree with them or defer to them in *their* domain. Then firmly stand behind the expertise in *your* domain that brought you into the room. In an ideal world, you would be able to come with a solution where each person has primary and secondary roles for different parts. Think of it as, "Let me do what I do well so you can continue to focus on what you do so well."

I've had a condescending peer from another organization not only request, but insist on reviewing my newsletters, be consulted on job roles I'm opening, and, in fact, even suggested the title I give to my leaders. I had unsolicited advice flying at me faster than bees to cake at a picnic. In each situation, I acknowledged his years of experience and successes in *his* domain and reminded him that I was brought in as an industry expert in *my* domain. I informed him that, although I appreciated his interest, the organization would slow down massively if we all had this level of oversight on each other. My own leadership chain didn't even want this level of involvement. Instead, I suggested quarterly check-in meetings where we could collaborate and provide *bi-directional* input. Collaboration is not "I'm going to do my own thing, but you have to do what I say."

Let's go back to the questions and comments from the beginning of this chapter. Clearly, they came from someone's Parent state, and the effect is diminishing. How do you elegantly pull the conversation back to an Adult-Adult state with confidence and facts? It sucks, and it's not really your job to explain your situation, but it's better to address these attitudes upfront with strength than to let them fester. Fight the temptation to be defensive. It may be more gratifying to release your fury in the moment, but it is much more rewarding to see the blank look on their face when your answer is so firm and clear that there is nothing more to say.

Question: How does it feel to get a job just because you're a *woman*?
Answer: I'm not sure what that feels like, but I'm sure it feels a lot better than when I *didn't* get considered because I'm a woman.

Statement: This is how things have always been.
Answer: Here is the state of affairs now and how it's changed and continuing to change. Let's talk about how we can work together to prepare for tomorrow.

Question: The "momsplain." How will you be able to raise your family while meeting the demands of a career?
Answer: I'm really resourceful. I have designed my life with the appropriate infrastructure to accommodate both.

Statement: The "mansplain."
Answer: Thank you for expanding on the idea that came from _____ *me, Nicole, George ... or whoever the originator is.*

This last one is especially important. Whether it's happening to you or someone else, when you see it, you gotta call it out.

We all have these ego states within us. What if you inadvertently trigger someone into a Child state? One of the easiest ways to do that is when it's time to provide feedback. When you have guidance to give, make sure it is specific, with an emphasis on outcome, rather than behavior. The behavior may directly affect the outcome, but let outcome be the primary factor. With my team, I will prepare them for it. "I have some feedback to offer that may help us improve … our relationship, the credibility of your brand, or the results we're both targeting." With my peers, I will ask for permission. "Would you be open to some observations?" I will always ask permission from my peers and especially of my superiors, because sometimes they're having a rotten day and they just don't feel like it, sometimes they're aware of their issues but they don't have the mental calories to deal with it yet.

If, however, it's not one person or one circumstance, there may be a fundamental cultural mismatch, and it might be time to bail. There is only so much you can do. Not every battle is worth it. As in love and poker, sometimes it's better to resist the sunk cost fallacy, which is the temptation to continue on a path in which you have already invested time, money, or effort. It's difficult to let go due to the loss aversion and status quo biases wired into the circuitry of our brains. Difficult, but not impossible, and we'll discuss this when we address risk taking.

The good news is that you have the power to make that choice, and you don't have to wait for someone else to make it for you. The bad news is that fearlessness not only requires courage, it requires being heard, which is in the control of your listener, not you. The ugly: you have to take accountability for your part of the transaction. The good news (positive me again): you can approach each interaction with the clarity of *your* purpose. Throughout my career, the seven-year-old surrounded by seven girls constantly weighs when to stand down and when to stand firm. Letting others put you in a box of inferiority is letting them steal your voice and suppress your creativity.

Think about situations that make you defensive and prepare how you would answer in your Adult state. Engage in a way that shows that you heard and considered the other point of view. If your counterpart feels heard, they will be much more compelled to listen to you, as well. If they have a better solution, great! If not, you have the right to present your case clearly and firmly without being defensive. If you can truly listen with open eyes and open ears, you can respond with an open heart and an open mind. And you can be received with the same. As Daya sings, you don't have to "*Sit Still, Look Pretty.*" You can rule your own world.

Chapter 6

Achieve Without Access

"Success doesn't come from what you do occasionally,
it comes from what you do consistently."

– Marie Forleo

On a recent vacation in Lake Tahoe, I listened to a MasterClass by Chris Voss, former FBI lead negotiator of international kidnapping and author of *Never Split the Difference*. Fascinated, I listened to it all the way through. Wishing I had learned his techniques in my 20s, I forced my teenagers to listen with me as we drove back to the Bay Area. A couple months later, I could barely contain my excitement to be invited to an intimate virtual happy hour with the master negotiator. He recalled his first phone conversation with the father of a 12-year-old boy who was kidnapped in Haiti. The distressed man asked him, "How are you going to help me?" Chris continued to explain the data on first impressions. How much time did he have to assure the father? The same that each of us has in every one of our interactions. Seven seconds. In that short time, "You have to establish two things: trust and competence."

Let's talk about trust. In Valerie Alexander's TEDxPasadena talk, *How to Outsmart Your Own Unconscious Bias*, the Founder and CEO of Goalkeeper Media, refers to the Dartmouth Undergraduate's Journal of Science article on the *Physiology of Stress*.

The most ancient part of the human brain, the amygdala, when it encounters the unexpected, it floods your system with stress hormones. Fight or flight is what kept our species alive for millions of years. None of us, in one hundred lifetimes, will ever be able to change that trigger *inside* our brains. So, our only solution is to change what's *outside* our brains. To consciously turn the unexpected into the expected so that we don't have unconscious hormonal reactions.

- Valerie Alexander

Well, crap. When someone encounters someone who's different from their usual experience, they're encountering the unexpected. Mistrust of misfits is biological. And the only way to fix it, is to flip the script. That's just great.

Why does this happen? According to *Encyclopedia Britannica*, the human body sends 11 million bits per second to the brain for processing, yet the conscious mind seems to be able to process only 50 bits per second. Our brains have developed coping mechanisms to manage all the information it has to process at any waking moment of the day. Snap judgements allow us to cut through irrelevant information to focus on key factors. Though I'm a fan of mastering thin-slicing to hone adaptive decision making, we have to be vigilantly aware of one pitfall—misplaced assumptions.

While growing up, there were many situations where I was the only minority in the room. If there were many minorities, I was often the only Asian. When I entered engineering, I started to see more variation in color, but less variation in gender. As I began climbing the corporate ladder, people who looked like me were disappearing. Looking above me for role models, variety fell off the cliff, leaving me hanging from the edge. I know what it's like to be different and to have people distrust your intentions or question your capability because of your uniqueness. Blue Skittles are regarded with suspicion. Strike one of two.

Let's talk about competence. As a person without access, it's more difficult, yet even more important, to establish a foundation of credibility. Lacking a network that will vouch for you, lacking the resources to build your extracurricular resume to get into the most reputable schools, or lacking the luxury to fund a few more years of education to earn a graduate degree can lead to a lack of consideration for career-changing opportunities. You are scrutinized more closely because it's harder to make it past these initial credibility filters. Shit. Strike two of two.

As a minority woman without access, you're already starting on the back foot. These two critical elements are harder to attain. Biology is conspiring against your trustworthiness, and lack of access is conspiring to pre-filter you from consideration. Difficult, but not impossible. Fortunately, meritocracy can get you pretty far along. Both of these considerations can be overcome with intelligence and diligence as an individual contributor. You can't control bias, but you can definitely control your output. This is where you put in the work to hone your craft and make your contribution undeniable. Demonstrated success will pave the way for trust and confidence.

My professional journey has taken quite a few twists and turns. At each crossroad, I had to earn the trust of someone who was willing to take a risk on my career changes from engineering to marketing, and eventually from entrepreneurship to sales. As an individual contributor, it was important to earn trust within my organization, as well as the functions we worked closely with. As an entrepreneur, my sales were a direct product of my brand reputation for marketing and sales consultation. As a leader in revenue enablement, I have the honor of driving significant transformation in today's digital economy.

In every role, it is important to build trust and inspire confidence in your competence. As an individual, how do you showcase your talent to drive impact? As an entrepreneur, how do you convince someone to invest in you? As a leader, how do you relieve anxiety of the masses to steward bold change? Be curious, establish credibility, and lead with courage. ***Earn it. Own it. Evolve it.*** There is no room for entitlement when you're asking teams within and without your organization to join you on a journey and adopt your vision, your roadmap, and your work ethic.

Curiosity. Credibility. Courage.

What do Benjamin Franklin, Albert Einstein, Steve Jobs, and Leonardo DaVinci all have in common? Each innovator was driven by a unique purpose, but with a common quality of mischievous ***curiosity*** that spanned the arts and sciences. Exploring their curiosities would make them experts in their respective fields and beyond. Benjamin Franklin was not only one of the most profound American political thinkers, he was an observer and a writer. Albert Einstein, who rebelled against regimented education systems that hampered his creativity, would develop the most elegant equation in physics, while being a self-taught violinist. Steve Jobs set out to "make a dent in the universe" by beautifully weaving technology and art into a canvas whose purpose was to "think differently." Each intellectual journey was captured in *The Genius Biographies* by University Professor of History at Tulane, Sir Walter Isaacson.

My favorite genius of these four has to be the historical misfit. An illegitimate, gay, ambidextrous vegetarian, Leonardo da Vinci was proud that his ineligibility for formal education forced him to learn from his own experiences instead. One of the most inventive minds in history persistently tested what Isaacson refers to as "received wisdom" from authorities to continuously learn and unlearn. That isn't to say that da Vinci discarded knowledge. He ingested data while allowing room for experimentation. When people justify their dismissal of education by comparing their out-of-the-box thinking to Einstein, Sir Walter Isaacson responds with, "He knew what was in the box before he could think out of it." You have to learn before you can unlearn.

It's not lost on me that these examples are based on four white men. In looking for role models, there are substantially more stories of white male heroes in history and pop culture. I look forward to the day when we can just as easily identify a series that celebrates minorities and *sheroes* with equal historical significance and reverence.

In the early years of my career, I won't lie, there were moments when I was completely petrified. Semiconductor engineering is hard. The end-to-end process is like baking a two-thousand-layer cake, one inch at a time, over a period of weeks. And the circuitry in this 2,000-layer cake? When I began, we were working with line widths of 0.8 microns, and by the time I left, we were at 0.25 microns (in comparison, a strand of human hair is 65 microns in diameter on average). It was even harder to keep up with the brain trust around me. My immediate peers held masters and PhDs in physics. I was totally in way over my head, but that's exactly why I loved that first job so much. The challenge was immense, and fortunately, my co-workers were generous and patient with me.

As the most junior engineer, it would have been easy to only be relegated to menial tasks, which I obviously fulfilled. But I also continuously asked for challenges and leaned into them with fervor. By showing the willingness to roll up my sleeves to do the grunt work as well as the hunger to solve hard problems, I was fortunate to have been entrusted with challenging experiments. Some went well. Some not so much. When I had a different opinion, I owned it. When I made mistakes, I owned those, too. I took lessons from failed experiments to design new ones. 'Cause science is awesome like that.

You win points by being bold. You don't have to keep your head down while you're learning. It can be incredibly intimidating to have a different opinion from a group of seasoned professionals, but that's where you bring value.

I could have just sat down and shut up in awe of my peers, but how does that add value? Fresh eyes may form unexpected hypotheses. I got really good at pattern matching, but I wanted to consume more data more efficiently and remove human decision making wherever possible. When I started, we tracked failures on paper and VAX notes, an early collaboration technology, and we made decisions by committee. I gradually replaced these systems with digital data structures and automated processes, for which I would receive multiple patents by the age of 30.

You win even more points when you step up to your mistakes. It shows the courage to bring your ideas to the table, self-awareness to recognize when things aren't working, and willingness to learn from your experiments. It shows curiosity. It shows passion. Have the courage to excel beyond executing flawlessly against your assignments by proactively bringing everything else you have in your toolkit to drive innovation. I may not have had an advanced degree, but I earned trust by playing at their level and showing my competence.

Allow yourself to be curious:
1. Learn from everywhere and everyone with insatiable curiosity and boundless humility.
2. Research. Experiment. Evaluate.
3. Have the vulnerability to challenge your own thinking.

Credibility is hard to earn, easy to lose, and harder still to recover. To earn credibility, you have to exhibit competence, consistency, and accountability.

At the beginning of my career, I managed teams of technicians at Advanced Micro Devices (AMD) while young, short, and female. As an Asian woman who just received her bachelor's degree, I looked like a 12-year-old child, hardly the vision of authority. As mentioned, my peers literally were brainiacs with advanced degrees, and many of my direct reports were at least twice my age. Everyone around me was some combination of smarter and more experienced than me. I was a blue Skittle. Respect would have to be earned.

The best way to change perception is to flip the script. Get the other person used to expecting the unexpected from you. Young professionals are stereotyped as inexperienced, yet arrogant and impatient. However, they're also recognized for their hunger and quick pace of learning. It was important to allay everyone's fears, while focusing on the characteristics they valued. And although Asian women are regarded as smart, they're generally expected to be meek and compliant. My height, or lack thereof, didn't help with that expectation, either. Well, there was nothing I could do about that.

By working alongside my team, I was able to immerse myself into their job roles. Earning my stripes showed our technicians the respect I had for the wealth of knowledge they possessed and empathy for their work. The team witnessed my youthful hunger and agile learning, but it was my lack of arrogance that disarmed them. There was no daily task too lowly that I didn't learn or couldn't help out with in a pinch.

I remember getting a page at 2 a.m. because one of our tools was misbehaving. In a 24/7 manufacturing environment, every minute of efficiency counts. With limited staff around at that odd hour, my team was desperate to get this machine running again. I came in groggy-eyed 20 minutes later, covered from head to toe in my cleanroom gear. After a preliminary system check, I took out a screwdriver and started crawling around and tearing apart a million-dollar tool, the size of a refrigerator, until I could find where the vacuum was disrupted. All of a sudden, my youth and other outlier statuses disappeared. I may have been part of the team, but I also happened to be the expert they could count on. They certainly didn't expect a dainty girl to be so handy. Every experience is useful. All those years spending time with my dad under cars and with my nose in engines made me unafraid of big machines. Even at 2 a.m. Even dressed like a scientist studying Ebola. Through the next few years, I would gain a reputation for reliability and ingenuity. I had earned their trust and confidence in my competence.

Just as Einstein had to know what was in the box before he could think out of it, you need to know yourself and your limitations in order to progress beyond them. In the workplace, you need to know your role really well. And if you don't, fake it till you make it. Put yourself in the shoes of your peers and the executives you support. What outcomes do they need from your function? Take the time to understand how you fit into the strategy and excel within your box before venturing outside of it. Otherwise, you won't be known for your talent, you'll only be known for being irritating.

To earn credibility, get really, really good at what you do:
1. Become relentlessly relevant by developing your expertise.
2. Become adept at pattern matching and situational analysis.
3. Make sure you can be counted on. Say what you do and do what you say. Consistently.

Courage is the ability to take action despite fear. It demands honesty and clarity of purpose.

Neither of my parents went to university. In fact, my mother quit school at the age of 12 to work alongside her mother, so her older brother and five younger siblings could finish their studies. Even without degrees, my parents earned their way to respectable statuses. My father led troops while my mother led schools. When they had to flee their world and start over, they overcame language and financial barriers to send eight children to college. Until all my siblings moved out, I can't remember a day when my dad wasn't fixing one of the used cars we had to shuttle all of us around.

Although my parents desperately wanted me to study medicine, the ultimate hallmark of prestige among Asians, I followed my analytical passions to study engineering. Midway through my college years, I considered transferring to business, to which my parents firmly replied, "You're Asian—doctor, lawyer, engineer—pick one." I guess I'm lucky that I didn't have the additional female limitation that my friends have faced, where the choices were, "Be a pharmacist, accountant, or another safe profession for a girl. Let the boys become the doctors and lawyers." Funnily enough, my friends from various ethnic backgrounds chuckle in empathy. Apparently, parental bullying into these fields is not a unique claim of the Vietnamese people.

Ironically, sometimes life insists on steering you toward your passions. Once seated in corporate life, I continued to watch the business decision makers rule the world. They studied the market and took guidance from customers to direct engineering priorities. The more I sat in executive meetings, the more I became interested in the business plan and revenue numbers. As much as I loved engineering, after a few years, I felt my experience had served its purpose, and I was ready to move closer to the business. I felt that familiar itch from college. I had the curiosity, but I definitely didn't have any credibility. The question was, did I have the courage to take such a hard left turn in my life? Time for introspection.

Reflect. I had a perfectly good life with my husband and moderate success for my age. Why was I doing this? Was it a fleeting moment of boredom? Was I ready to disappoint my parents further?

Recalibrate. If the urge I had in college had not left me, and in fact only gotten stronger, the feeling was not likely to go away. The sands had shifted. If I really thought about it, my parents were generous souls who ultimately just wanted me to be secure and happy. At this point, they had witnessed my ability to stand on my own, despite my frustratingly stubborn and unconventional approach to life. They would trust me to find my happiness. If I denied my calling, I knew that continuing success in a profession I had outgrown would leave me empty, and who would that serve?

Reset. I had to remember the regret of not applying to McKinley Middle School. I had to remember that I didn't know anything about making microchips when I started my career. There's no point in self-selecting out. If only I could find someone to take a chance on me in marketing or sales, I would figure it out. Women are known for suffering from imposter syndrome, convincing themselves of being frauds and attributing their successes to luck. Can you think of some examples of when you quit before you even started? What were the limiting beliefs and excuses you made?

Credibility begets credibility. One of the most challenging interviews I've ever had in my life was making the transition from engineering at AMD to marketing at Cisco Systems. I didn't have the education or experience. Instead, I did my homework. I studied the basics of networking, beginning with the OSI model (the seven layers of Open Systems Interconnection), and I studied the basics of marketing. In the interview, I referenced the business meetings I attended at AMD, the perspectives I brought as an engineer, perspectives I learned from marketing that broadened my narrow point of view and sparked epiphanies in areas I wanted to learn. That manager would tell me decades later that he hired me for my tenacity and creative thinking. What I thought was borderline desperation, he found absolutely courageous.

Why would a chemical engineer end up in network infrastructure sales? I like to say that "I started in engineering because I like numbers and I like solving complex problems. I made my way to sales because, apparently, I have a preference for numbers with dollar signs in front of them." My curiosity would take me down a winding path that included almost 10 years in engineering, 10 years in marketing, and the last 10 years in sales. I didn't know it at the time, but following my curiosity would give me the broad experience that I would eventually need to be successful in a role that touches all these disciplines.

Curiosity requires the confidence to be vulnerable. To acknowledge that you don't have all the answers. To pause and ask "Why?" I was, and still am the nerd at the front of the room asking way too many questions. I'm the kid who finds a loose corner of wallpaper and just keeps peeling. My chemical engineering curriculum didn't prepare me for a career in semiconductor manufacturing among physicists. It took more than seven seconds, but I established trust and competence. Years later, I transitioned to marketing and sales without a business degree. I got my MBA by OJT (on-the-job training). Not all learning is academic. I learned from books, from people, and from direct experience. It took more than seven seconds, but I established trust and competence there, too. The blue Skittle can find a way to get accepted, after all.

Earn it. Own It. Evolve it.

In *The Shadow Man: a Daughter's Search for Her Father*, Mary Gordon writes, "A fatherless girl thinks all things possible and nothing safe." I think it applies to anyone who experiences grief, and especially those who experience loss at a tender age. Fear of the fleeting has made me cognizant of the impermanence of security, motivated me to earn my place in the world, and inspired me to help others along their own journey.

Earn it. I have long embraced my stereotypical Asian nerdiness. Being academically competitive, I was always aware that achievements are temporary, and earning a spot does not give me the right to keep it. Even as a product of one of the lowest-rated public school systems in the country, I learned how to learn without access and the importance of staying sharp and agile. This is a skill I have come back to frequently along my circuitous career path. Being smart is not enough. You have to do the work to get really damn good at what you do so your talent can help you navigate your obstacles. Today, I earn my seat with my engineering skills for complex problem solving, and marketing and sales skills to connect with customers. What experience can you leverage and what skills do you need to add to your toolkit?

Own it. Own the privilege of your responsibility to serve your stakeholders every day. Like the 1989 movie, *Field of Dreams* asserts, if you build it, they will come. Build a good product or process with competence, consistency, and accountability, and you will be recognized as the expert. As an entrepreneur, this reputation is what convinces someone to invest in you. As a leader, this reputation is what inspires the masses to follow your vision.

Do you remember the irritating peer who wanted to approve my newsletters and have input into my organizational structure? I kept smiling and nodding. I couldn't control his actions and inputs. I could only control my reactions and output. I kept building a great program. I didn't have to self-accolade, I let my reputation precede and follow me. Eventually, recognition from other teams outside of my organization isolated and quelled any sound of negativity my colleague attempted to propagate.

Evolve it. Albert Einstein is credited with defining insanity as doing the same thing and expecting different results. In today's head spinning pace of innovation, the corollary is if you're not ahead of the curve, you're falling behind it. The reality is that business has forever changed and will only continue to pick up speed. With digital disruption, we are already slower today than we will be tomorrow. Keeping up requires continuous learning and evolution. Have the courage to drive a culture that aspires to an ever-progressing definition of excellence.

No one can innovate alone. My diverse experience also allows me to empathize with my colleagues' point of view and respect their expertise. If you don't have that breadth of experience, find or build a team with cognitive diversity. Race, gender, age, tenure, professional and artistic backgrounds, bring 'em *all* to the table. Collaborate widely to crowdsource ideas that will help you consistently deliver creative solutions. Create platforms for conversation. We all have our gifts and our gaps. Embrace the strength of others to complement your own and embrace the power of the collective to design the best programs. In this way, we can build trust and competence not only as individuals, but as an organization. We are truly better together. Follow the song from the Chicks to expand the horizon for everyone and find *"Wide Open Spaces"* where "a young girl's dreams" are "no longer hollow."

Chapter 7
Take Your Expectations Off Road

"It ain't what you don't know that gets you into trouble.
It's what you know for sure that just ain't so."

– Mark Twain

A classic interview question is: What advice would you give a younger version of yourself? I would send up huge flares about following formulas for success that were not written for me. I would blow up the myths of meritocracy when navigating the murky middle. I would highlight the pitfalls of pursuing perfection. I would force my younger self to find a way to play the game of life with energetic authenticity, rather than self-selecting out with arrogant disdain.

When you start a journey, how do you pick your destination and how do you plan your route? Do you print out a paper map and stay on the path, no matter what? Or do you follow a route that someone else has written for you on a map they've drawn for you? Have you ever stopped for directions, only to realize after someone eagerly guides you, that they're pointing the wrong way?

We put so much pressure on ourselves to have the world figured out in our 20s. Then we willingly hold ourselves hostage to those simplistic beliefs for decades thereafter, even when our circumstances and beliefs change. What if there's somewhere else you want to go? What if there are obstructions along the way? Constraining yourself to a stagnant picture that only captures a single moment in time limits your ability to adjust for disruptions. The path you've plotted at the beginning isn't necessarily the course you're meant to take for the rest of your life.

If I were to provide guidance, it would be to focus less on a single destination. Instead, let your purpose be your North Star, and give yourself the grace to course-correct along the way. Set a trajectory, but give yourself 1, 2, or 5-year goals versus 20 to 50-year goals. This will give you the space to constantly *reflect, recalibrate,* and *reset* to honor the path of your authentic self and take the life-defining risks necessary to get you from here to wherever "there" may be.

I followed the playbook until I didn't. I worked hard for a great education, went to university, got a good job, got married, bought a house, and had a couple babies. Then at some point, I started veering off the path farther and farther until I was no longer even on the small map with which I began. What critical choices were made along the way? What were the decision criteria? And what flexibility was required in response to circumstances as they emerged?

In a 1943 publication of *Psychological Review*, Abraham Maslow discussed *A Theory of Human Motivation*. Maslow's psychological theory of the hierarchy of human needs is often depicted as five tiers in a pyramid. Table-stakes needs lower down in the hierarchy must be satisfied before individuals can attend to a higher pursuit. This means that the lower, more critical levels may take precedence over the higher levels *at any point in time.* From the broad base of the triangle upwards toward the pinnacle, the needs are:

1. Physiological (food, water, shelter)
2. Safety (security of health and property)
3. Belonging (family, friends, intimacy)
4. Esteem (achievement, confidence, respect)
5. Self-actualization (acceptance and creativity to realize one's potential)

For many immigrants, mere survival is marked as the destination because joy is perceived as a luxury. This hyper-focus on basic needs can lead to an inflexible life map. I encourage those who began without access to practice self-acceptance. Survival does not have to come at the cost of suffering; it can actually transcend into fulfilment of the highest need, the freedom for self-actualization.

Maslow's model explains why it's much harder to disaggregate personal stories from professional choices for women. If we refer back to binary societal expectations, men are typically expected to be the primary breadwinner. That makes him responsible for the first two layers of Maslow's hierarchy: food, water, shelter, security. This means that *his* career and ambition take precedence over *any other* consideration, *at any given time*. If a woman's primary role is to be a nurturer, she's responsible for creating belonging, turning a house into a home. She provides for family, friends, and community. In these traditionally prescribed roles, each character would find their next level of need, esteem, in their respective roles as primary provider or caregiver.

How then does a woman justify her ambitions, especially if it requires sacrifices by her family? In doing so, is she being a selfish bitch? If her husband is supportive and agrees to step back on providing in order to step up on caregiving, is he being an irresponsible, spineless wimp? When we're young, we tend to follow or rebel against the examples set before us. As emerging adults, we start figuring out how to resolve who we are going to be as we leave the nest. Provider, caregiver, or some combination thereof? I made a conscious decision to include very personal stories here because all of my personal decisions impacted my career and vice versa. As a woman especially, personal expectations and professional goals are intricately intertwined.

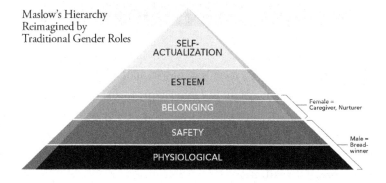

A Conventional Path Followed by Unconventional Choices

Learning from my middle school experience to opt-in to stellar programs, I jumped on an opportunity in college to alternate semesters of school with semesters of paid internship. Beginning with a co-op program at the age of 19, I continued with AMD beyond graduation until I was only six months shy of eligibility for a highly revered benefit: a two-month sabbatical after seven years of service. Not only did I leave substantial paid time off, I left my parentally-approved engineering job. This marketing role was a perceived step down in prestige in my culture and the 20 percent pay cut was a concrete step down in my bank account. Sorry, Mom and Dad.

After some very rewarding years in engineering, no matter the cost, it was time for me to take the next fork in the road to follow my authentic joy. For two years, I searched within and without the company. The best option I could find was as a sales engineer for semiconductor vendors. Even then, opportunities in the Austin market were few and far between. My husband was supportive during the years I was interviewing for roles within Austin, but became distressed when I began interviewing out of state.

When I bit the bullet and accepted a job at the center of the high-tech universe in Silicon Valley, my husband was not amused. He was born and raised in Dallas. We had only been married for five years, and we had barely spent three years in our new house on our multi-acre lot in north-central Austin. In his view, "if it ain't broke, don't fix it," life was already good. This new twist highly disrupted our meticulously mapped out plan to spend the rest of our lives within miles of where we first met. The expensive housing, notorious traffic, and general unfamiliarity of California were not appealing to him. And don't forget the earthquakes. Unpredictable weather, tornadoes, and golf-ball-sized Texas hail we understood, but earthquakes?

On the other hand, I was professionally, and therefore personally, miserable. Layer on top of that the shame of "wanting more." My family thought I was nuts. Why move to expensive California where I had no family? For immigrants, we already have so much more than our parents could have wanted for us. Why did I need so much? How much would be enough? My husband's mother was really upset that I was forcing her son into unfamiliar territory. I was upsetting everyone around me who cared about me. I had some significant soul searching to do.

Reflect. My husband, Bob, had a point, we had everything already. According to Maslow's hierarchy of needs, we were doing really well.

- Layers 1 & 2: Physiological safety and security. *We were comfortable and safe. Check. Check.*
- Layer 3: Belonging. *We had a community of friends, regular dinners with my family in Austin, and spent holidays only a few hours away with his family in Dallas. Check.*
- Layer 4: Esteem. *We were succeeding according to our life plan. Check.*
- Layer 5: Self-actualization. *Reaching my potential. Why was this even necessary? Why couldn't we just live like this forever? Why did the rules have to change?*

Recalibrate. Bob wasn't wrong, but in my gut, I knew I wasn't wrong, either. Everyone deserves their definition of happiness, and our paths were simply starting to diverge. I wanted to change the world. I wanted to embrace my edge and show little girls like my daughter and my 11 nieces what they could do, and that would mean leading by example. I wanted to show little boys like my son and my six nephews the exhilaration of endless possibilities when the opposite sex is an equal partner. When you're that dissatisfied, you can't be the best person you can be. I was not the most wonderful wife, and we separated for a few months.

Reset. This was not the way to live. I was already unhappy, and we were already apart. Screw the earthquakes. I planned to relocate first and give my husband the space to follow when he felt comfortable, knowing there was an inherent risk that he would do neither.

Nine days before the moving truck was scheduled to swoop me away, my husband decided to follow me, after all. He asked his boss at the Austin site of Cisco Systems for referrals to transfer to San Jose headquarters. When he relayed our background and my motivation, his director immediately connected us to the local marketing department. James Collinge, the DSL product line manager and a fellow veteran of semiconductors, had a junior position open. His own experience at Texas Instruments gave him an appreciation for the complex understanding required in that industry, which made him much more amenable to hiring for intelligence and potential over direct experience. He was willing to take a gamble on me.

I stayed in Austin and joined Cisco in the summer of 2000. My husband and I reconciled. The dot com world would begin unravelling six months after that. What was once a plethora of jobs competing for limited talent disappeared quickly on a dime. Had I waited, I would have likely missed a rare opportunity to transition from engineering to marketing *and* switch industries at the same time. For audiences outside of technology, that gobbledy-gook may not seem like a huge leap, but for those on the inside, it's the difference between apples and onions.

Even *if* I would eventually be able to make both transitions, it would have taken an extra step, and a few years in between. More likely though, I would have gotten discouraged, kept my head down, and plodded along for another 30 years in the same place, collecting the same two-month break every seven years. When asked why I took that leap of faith, I couldn't explain it. All I knew was that my unconscious always sensed it in my gut. It would be years later that I would learn of the brain science behind decision making, and the search for balance between logic and instinct.

Seize opportunities before the window closes. My parents had no idea they would flee a country. While others chose to stay behind in the comfort of familiarity, they took a calculated risk. On a much smaller scale, I never expected to have such a large responsibility at a global company. In fact, I never even knew I wanted it. If you have an urge, do not self-select out of a path you have yet to take.

To the outside world, leaving an engineering management role for a more junior role in marketing was a professional step down. I didn't think twice, not even for a nanosecond. I wasn't interested in a job. I was interested in following my purpose. I wanted to pursue a career in a field where I could grow, in a company with undeniable brand recognition. But why not wait just a few short months to at least enjoy the time off? And why do it for a significant pay cut? Simple. This was my "trusting the stranger to throw the baby onto the boat" moment. The deeply embedded stories of the war instilled a sense of urgency and potential loss. As a result, my fear of stagnation is much greater than my fear of the unknown. I can literally almost feel walls closing in on me, personal growth hampered, a metaphorical suffocation of my intellectual soul. That may be a little dramatic, but you get the idea.

Six years later, we would revisit the conversation about moving to California again, under very different circumstances. Bob knew I was still itching to move to California, so he entertained a job with Google. Of course, I was supportive of him and excited for the possibility to move to the Bay Area. How do you think my family and his family received this news? All of a sudden, they were very supportive. It was, after all, a valiant move for the head of household to secure Layer 1 of Maslow's hierarchy. I would be lying if I didn't say my insides weren't on fire at the unfairness. As a good wife, I swallowed my pride and continued to smile and nod. I kicked the can down the road. My husband didn't get the job, so it didn't become a big conversation. Until it did.

Losing Daddy

That fall, it was nearing Halloween when my son was in soccer practice at Coach Richard's house. My husband and I were playing cards with other parents when I received a call from my father. He informed me that he had advanced liver cancer. An immediate fog filled my brain while tears filled my eyes. I remember stepping into the brisk October air to talk about his prognosis and how to deliver the message to the rest of the family. His responses were vague when I asked him what stage he was in and how much longer he had left. I sighed heavily and leaned against the car for balance as he simply asked me to tell the family not to worry and that every remaining day would be a gift.

A good number of my siblings and I were able to spend a very special Thanksgiving with him. Having spent the holidays with him and my in-laws in Dallas, I went to visit my mother in Orange County in January. She left my father when I was 16 to "take care of the grandchildren" and never came home. Back in Austin, my sister called me on a Thursday to tell me that Daddy didn't sound right. I called him and figured out he had gone to his first chemotherapy session by himself without telling any of us and was suffering immensely in the aftermath. I took the first plane I could to Dallas Friday morning and spent the next few days with his doctors, sifting through his records to understand the gravity of the situation.

On Friday, I went through all of his medication, and I was alarmed to find he never filled the post-chemo prescription. Why? Because each pill was $700. He never told us. In the meantime, I found a stack of checks on his dresser that all of the kids had given him over the holidays, amounting to over $10,000, which he couldn't bear to cash. This is what immigrant children do, and this is what immigrant parents do. His roommate of 18 years had also been sick with bone cancer for the past year. On his kitchen table stood about 30 vials of her pills, lined up neatly in rows. I was out of my mind to find he had been self-medicating ineffectively with oxycodone, a narcotic painkiller, in place of an anti-nausea medication.

When I took him to the doctor that evening, I found out his cancer was already at stage IV. When I asked about the medication, the doctor told me it was so expensive because it was an experimental drug that wasn't covered by insurance. He said he wished he had known my dad was in such a tight spot and proceeded to give my father four days' worth of samples. For free. Without understanding the system, my dad didn't know the right questions to ask.

That night, I organized a family conference call. The eight of us talked for hours as I gave everyone an assessment of his medical state. For the next two days, I drove the twenty-five miles back and forth from my in-laws to my dad's house in the middle of an ice storm. I didn't self-select out at work; I'll be damned if I self-selected out of helping my dad before it was too late. I would drive five miles per hour if I had to in order to sort this out. The next day, I spent hours sitting on his living room floor with my lawyer on speakerphone, documenting my daddy's last wishes. But the ice closed down any notaries that would have even been open on a Saturday. I'd have to return to Dallas on a weekday to finalize the documents.

That second evening, I held my dad's hand as he moaned in pain, "If this is living, I'd rather die." With the deterioration of his liver, his belly was distended and full of fluid, compressing his organs. When the pain subsided, we talked for hours about his regrets, secrets, and life lessons—clarifying conversations we should have had years earlier. I realized that I held on to misplaced anger at a man who couldn't show up as his best self at home because he held onto outdated values that kept him from living his personal life authentically. Instead, he immersed himself where he could find joy, in his career. This avoidance made him disengaged and mean at home, while he was able to be kind and generous in the community.

As much as you try to shield them, kids feel the repercussions of their parents' unhappiness in their bones. They may not know what it is in their youth, but they *feel* it. As adult children, we have to be able to accept that our parents are fallible humans. As parents, we have to model for our own children that it's okay to course-correct your path, so that they in turn can grow up to make unconventional choices without shame. Love your children enough to show them who you really are, who and what you really love, before you land on your deathbed. I wish my dad had given me the opportunity to let him know that I would have been happier if he followed his own happiness.

While we had our heart-to-heart, it dawned on me that my dad had been making an effort to get close to us in his last 15 years. But as stubborn children, we all quietly held onto our own resentment. In that moment, I let go of all of it. I told him I understood how difficult his path had been, too, and he completely fell apart in relief that he was finally loved unconditionally. It is a humbling sight to watch your 77-year-old father, a proud military leader, cry like a baby. I left for the evening, just as the priest arrived to give him his last rites.

Once back at my in-laws, I dialed into another long conference call. Everyone was well-meaning, but with that many people under stress, you're just going to get a lot of opinions. My emotional calories were depleted, my patience frayed, and I had a low tolerance for being expected to listen to "ordained authority" from afar directing me on what to do and how to do it. In my view, being the boots on the ground gave me "organic authority." After a lifetime of being the respectful little sister, I found my voice as an equal among my siblings, despite being the youngest member and female. We created a schedule of who would call Daddy each day, at which time, and who would come visit him every week for the next nine weeks. Exhausted, I hung up the phone and cried myself to sleep.

The next day, when I went to visit him again, he was the most lucid I had seen him. We had brunch and laughed. He lectured me about diet and exercise. I rolled my eyes. Things had almost gotten back to normal. I taped the call and visitation schedule that my family had agreed upon onto the wall next to the phone, and I taped his daily medication schedule under that sheet. He couldn't have been happier to see that his estranged children were rallying to visit and take care of him. I gave him a kiss on the cheek as I headed for the airport to go home to Austin and told him I would be back next Friday to get his will and other legal paperwork notarized.

When I landed a couple hours later, there was already a voicemail on my phone from my dad's housemate's son. He was frantic. Daddy had collapsed and the ambulance had taken him away. On the taxi ride home, I called my husband to tell him to get the car and the kids ready. I would be home in 20 minutes to pick them up and drive back to Dallas. Night was falling and more freezing rain was on its way. Ignoring concerns from my siblings for my safety, I knew we had a small window of time before we would "miss the boat" before the storm. I felt the urgency at my core. Roads were closing behind us as we made the trek north. As soon as the family was in the car and my husband was driving, my oldest sister and I dialed into the emergency room to let the doctor know that my father had a Do Not Resuscitate order. Solemnly, he asked us to authorize over the phone the withdrawal of the machines that would leave my dad's heart and lungs to fail naturally.

We finally made it to the hospital a little after midnight on January 16, 2007. My husband dropped me off to join my sister, Phuong (who drove in from nearby Plano), at my father's bedside. He was intubated and highly medicated, with a single tear at the corner of his closed eyes. As much as I would wipe it away, it would keep reforming there for hours, breaking my heart that he was still in pain. My dad loved football, so my sister and I watched a replay of a game on cable. I don't remember the teams playing, but I remember whispering play by plays in his ear, interspersed with telling him how much the family loved him, until his heart stopped beating a little past 7 a.m. My brother had flown all night from California, only to arrive an hour after the doctor called time of death. Time was of the essence, and only two of us made it in time to be by his side. The rest of my siblings arrived hours and days after that.

That weekend, my father and I forgave each other as I watched him die. In his last three days, I realized that I was repeating his mistakes. I realized how similar I was to a man I had spent a lifetime judging by a stubborn attachment to other people's values. I had to consider that my kids were young enough that I could adjust my own life before perpetuating the same cycle. I took ownership of my unhappiness.

It required me to *reflect* on my arrogance of believing I knew the formula for success at the age of 22. This was the moment that I compared who I had become to the 2002 projection of myself, who was planning on retiring when I had four children. It was difficult to admit I was blindly following a conventional story laid out before me, rather than pursuing my personal definition of success and happiness.

It was time to *recalibrate*. The death of my father exacerbated an itch for achievement that I had been unconsciously suppressing for years. When he left us, his impact was honored by busloads of immigrants he had helped over decades, who arrived from Baton Rouge, Louisiana to Arlington, Texas to pay their last respects. We were surprised when a local chapter of veterans marched in with their colors to give him an honorable, departing salute. This is what success meant to me: a career of service, becoming a role model, and touching other lives along the way.

I had to *reset* my own expectations. My career had begun stalling with the birth of my first child, which only inflamed my need for achievement. The Motherhood Penalty is real. We'll talk more in depth about that later. In the meantime, I had to resist the urge to apologize to the universe for my ambition, as if that simple act could erase the flaw. I had to decide if I had the fortitude to defy society's expectations of me, which meant choosing to cultivate, rather than suffocate, the painful seeds of growth that were blossoming within me. My father's death gave me the courage to finally move from Texas to California, to be closer to both my mother and to the land of innovation.

Surviving the drama of taking care of everyone else gave me the permission to turn my attention to my own needs as a person and a professional. It was time for a new chapter. As women and as immigrants, so many decisions in our professional lives are subservient to personal expectations from all around us—cultural expectations of familial obligations to our aging parents and grandparents, societal expectations, our husband's expectations, our children's expectations, and even our own expectations to follow the model. That's the challenge. As women and as immigrants, we feel pressured to ensure that we enable everyone else to play their roles, before we are allowed to venture out beyond our own confined limits.

As it happened seven years prior, I planned to relocate, knowing it was a decision that would strain my marriage. When you keep kicking the can down the road, guess what? At some point you're gonna trip on it. You might even fall over and break your face. Pick it up. Deal with your shit. If it had not been for that moment of courage, I would not have found my heart in San Diego. I would not have been invited to join the board of directors and eventually elected vice-chair of an international school. Those years working with accomplished executives, entrepreneurs, and lawyers at the top of their game to run a school gave me access to immense executive experience. Without that experience, I would not have learned to take the voice I found within my family and started exercising it in my professional life. Most importantly, if I had not moved, I would not have discovered the love of my life, my authentic self. I can hear Whitney Houston singing to me, "Learning to love yourself, it is the *Greatest Love of All.*"

Chapter 8
Surrender to the Suck

"We delight in the beauty of the butterfly but rarely admit the changes it has gone through to achieve that beauty."

– Maya Angelou

In the fall of 2006, right before I received the initial news about my father's cancer, a vice president at my company was changing roles. I wasn't in his organization, but he witnessed my work peripherally. In his move, he specifically asked for only two people out of hundreds: a director who already worked for him and me. I begged not to be moved because I had already established a good reputation with the leadership in my current business unit, and I was hoping to get promoted. I knew that going into a new department with new leaders would set the clock back in gaining credibility, at best. I also knew that starting over would put me at risk when it was time for the next round of layoffs, at worst. No go. The executive absolutely needed my irreplaceable operational skills. No choice. No voice. No promotion.

I could not control the company's actions and input; I could only control my reactions and output. Trying to mitigate my risk and maintain my visibility when the company cut all internal travel, I continued to fly up to headquarters from Texas at my own expense every month. Peons don't protest, after all. This is not how immigrants are raised. We sit down and shut up. But I controlled what I could. After my father's death, I moved to San Diego to be closer to my mother, and to be more accessible to headquarters. No matter. My prediction came to be.

The VP was struggling to establish his own footing with a new general manager who already had his set of trusted leaders. Within months, I was forgotten and abandoned and put on the dreaded "list." I had the unpleasurable experience of layoff #1. I had never, *ever, EVER* failed professionally before. I understood all the reasons, but I still took it personally. Two years later, I ran into that same VP, who was now a CEO of another company, at an industry event. When I greeted him, he didn't even know my name. Sometimes you may have the skill and the will, but you also need to have the circumstance.

When these things occur in large companies, you generally get two weeks to find a new job or plan for your exit. Names of those affected spread quickly, like gossip in high school. Directors who had worked with me before called upon their network to figure out where there might be an opening I could move into. Fortunately, a leader from another area of the organization swooped in to rehire me within 24 hours of hearing that I was getting let go. It didn't matter that I had never done the work he needed. Suraj Shetty, VP of Marketing, had witnessed my competence years ago, when I first joined Cisco. He trusted that I would figure it out. Years ago, my husband introduced me to his company, providing me "privileged access" that would enable me to change careers. This experience with Suraj would be my first lesson in "earned access," for which I am forever grateful. This opportunity wasn't handed to me. This access came from years of building a reputation for hard work and capability. It was a lesson I missed at the time, but I would draw on many times later in my career.

Determined not to get into this situation again and in gratitude to Suraj, I worked even harder. For two years, I contributed to writing the company's earnings reports, and for two years after that, I ran some of the company's largest trade shows that led to record-breaking year over year increases.

In the meantime, after moving to San Diego, I joined the board of my children's international school. During my tenure, the bright minds on the board took some bold risks and made some sweeping changes. Collectively, the new approaches we took increased the school's fundraising from a 23-year average of $15,000 to $160,000 within four years. At the same time, we increased parent participation from 13 percent to 52 percent within three years. But my ambition at work and at home took a toll on my relationship and my body. The reality is that cracks in my marriage started showing up the moment I started veering off the plan in Austin.

Epiphany in a Taxi to the Emergency Room

On Memorial weekend of 2008, I doubled over in the most pain I had ever felt in my life, much worse than laboring to deliver my nearly nine-pound son. My stomach felt like someone put a vice on it from the inside ... and lit it on fire. I remember writhing on my living room floor, basked in the moonlight coming through the picture window that framed the hills of La Jolla. I was unsure of what this was, what to do, or who to call while I was alone with two toddlers asleep upstairs.

My husband was at a conference in Chicago, and I had few friends, as we had just moved at the beginning of the school year. After a few hours of excruciating pain, I called another mom from my four-year-old daughter's class, whose husband was a heart surgeon. At 2 a.m., Martha put her husband on the phone. Matthew advised me to go to the emergency room immediately. My friend compassionately came to my house to watch my kids so I could take a cab to get myself to the hospital. This was the rock bottom that forced me to check my expectations of success. I had everything, I was alone, and I was miserable.

The stomach pain was the physical manifestation of an unbearable eighteen months in the school of life. After burying my father, my husband and I stretched our finances to buy a house in a competitive southern California market. We could not have had worse timing. Two months later, the real estate bubble burst, beginning the great recession. The person who put an offer on our Austin house earlier that summer decided to sue us in order to back out of the purchase. Shortly afterward, bad drainage in our new neighborhood caused a landslide that swallowed three homes nearby. Although we were safe, the proximity devastated our property value. That Halloween, we experienced our first California wildfires that were close enough for us to see the flames from our back deck and to smell the smoke from inside the house.

During that holiday season, we went back to Texas for two weeks and returned to find that our house had been burglarized. The criminals smashed a side window in the back of the house, entered the living room, opened our garage, and backed their truck in to give themselves ample time. Every single drawer had been overturned. Remnants of two fingertips of blue latex gloves were among the disarray. Every painting was taken down from the walls. Every single piece of jewelry I owned, including my engagement ring and an heirloom bracelet my mother passed on to me as a wedding gift, was taken. I had collected a bag of photos and memories to make a collage of me and my dad. Gone.

Reflect. When I looked in the mirror on that lonely taxi ride to the emergency room, I didn't recognize myself. I was completely broken. If this was life-school, I was in dire need of summer vacation. At home, my life was a wreck. My husband was as homesick for Texas as I was hungry to stay in California. Despite the caliber of my work product, my career had hit a wall for five years that I couldn't figure out how to break through. After being admitted, I had to drink this gooey concoction that amounted to a mixture of Maalox and Lidocaine. That was pleasant. After recovering for a couple of hours, I checked myself out and got in another cab back home.

The painful isolation was necessary to force me to surrender to the suck in order to find the strength to get out of it.

Recalibrate. A few weeks later, this same pain occurred again. But fortunately, my husband was home to take me to the ER this time, with our children in the backseat. Over the next few months, I would go to various doctors, who couldn't find anything wrong, except to determine that it was severe stress. Clearly, this was not sustainable. I had everything—a husband, kids, a career—and yet I was alone in my emptiness. Something had to change. It was time to review my definition of success, regardless of how unacceptable I feared it would be to those around me.

- *Significance:* From *fulfillment to prestige*—I cared less about the external accolades that I had been raised to seek. I yearned for the fulfillment of following my purpose and driving impact.
- *Security:* From *basic needs to luxurious wealth*—we were more financially comfortable than most. I didn't need more, and I would easily trade increased wealth for the significance I desired.
- *Stability:* From *familiarity to adventure*—I could no longer deny my need for continuous growth. As a child of war and grief, not much scares me. But for me, the pain of paralysis is much greater than the fear of the unknown.

Reset. As much as we loved each other, my husband and I picked up the can, dealt with our shit, and split up. But we chose to do so authentically, lovingly, and generously—not just for our children, but for ourselves as fellow humans who had been best friends for 16 years.

After my divorce, the company's escalating cadence of layoffs made me nervous. As a single mother, I felt extremely vulnerable. Trying to mitigate my risk and maintain my visibility, I packed up the kids and moved to the Bay Area in the summer of 2012. My children, who were seven and nine at the time, loved San Diego. When they asked why we were moving, I told them, "Mommy has been stuck in kindergarten for a long time. I'd like to skip middle school and high school in my job and go to college." They got on board. My ex-husband, who was now a loving co-parent, was able to transfer his job in order to follow us a few months later.

Wash. Rinse. Repeat.

Within six months of my move to the Bay Area, Cisco centralized my function from one organization to another. After running an overwhelmingly successful program, I received a hand-signed letter of appreciation from the CEO and four of the highest level awards from vice presidents in four separate areas of the company: service provider sales, mobility sales, engineering, and marketing. Shockingly, the next corporate letter I received a few days later informed me of layoff #2. My boss teared up when he called me. "You deserve a promotion. I don't know what to say except, I'm so sorry." Feeling his pain, I replied calmly, "I know. I trust you. I know you did everything you could for me. Are you okay? What can I do for you?" He choked up then, and still does whenever we reminisce about that moment. After hanging up the phone, I went for a run and cried the entire three miles. Several senior vice presidents called to tell me they had loudly exchanged some very choice words with the ranking executive that required her doors to be closed.

Again, within 48 hours, I received offers from two of the four leaders who recently awarded me the highest level of recognition. I could not control the company's action and inputs; I could only control my reaction and output. Time to kick professional development into high gear. What the hell was I doing wrong? Two points does not a pattern make, but it certainly wasn't good. One of the offers was to go back into the product side of the business, and the other was to work in sales. Disoriented, I consulted with a long-time mentor, Kelly Ahuja, Senior VP / General Manager of the Service Provider business. He knew of my love of sales, but he also knew my confidence had been completely shaken. He told me, "You just haven't had the opportunity to shine yet. Keep taking risks." With that encouragement, I went to work for his peer. Up for a new challenge and in gratitude to my new boss, I worked harder as a chief of staff in sales. That year, my performance earned me the best bonus and raise I had received since 2002.

In parallel, I sought mentoring and feedback from all corners—books, seminars, executives, and peers. Some resources I found useful, but a lot of advice for women I found conflicting and sometimes downright weird. Be assertive, but not aggressive. Be confident, but not arrogant. Be approachable, but not familiar. What the hell? Do men get coached with such opposing instructions? Never mind. I tried it all, anyway.

In 2013, my vice president called me privately. He was changing roles, and of his large organization, he only wanted to take two people. My director and me. Sound familiar? I voiced my history and concerns. That promotion I've been working on since my first layoff in 2007? It still had not happened because of the lack of longevity I had in any one seat to build the sponsorship I needed. No matter. The executive absolutely needed my irreplaceable business acumen. No choice. No voice. No promotion.

My previous experience validated my belief that you don't just have to win over the leader, you have to win over all the leaders above, around, and underneath them. I was terrified to start over. Yet again. But this time, I knew my VP. He didn't recruit me purely by reputation like the last one. I had already earned his trust in my competence. In fact, he had "saved" me from my second layoff, *and* in my first year with him, he had given me the best raise I received in a decade. Most importantly, I knew he would remember my name. Unlike last time, I was wary, but I had faith. Until I met my new boss. She was the most insecure, worst people manager I had ever encountered in my entire career, even to this day.

I was so unhappy, and I knew where this path would lead. I had seen this movie. In those last two years, I was quietly interviewing within and without Cisco. Within the company, I tried to move into a quota carrying sales role. Although impressed, the sales leaders wanted someone with sales experience. Each referred me to another peer and asked me to come back in six months after cutting my teeth with someone who might be willing to invest the time. No one took that gamble. Outside of the company, I ran into dead end after dead end. With Cisco's notorious annual layoff, companies questioned if I had survived that long because I was good at my job or if I was good at hiding in a giant company. I hadn't appropriately established a personal brand or a network outside of Cisco. Without allies and advocates to vouch for my skills, I had no access.

Losing Mommy

In the fall of 2015, I was hiking among the waterfalls in Oregon with my children and ex-husband when I received a call from my oldest sister. At 87 years old, my mother had a heart attack. With the same urgency I had with my father, I flew back to Orange County the next day. This time, my siblings mobilized quickly, enabling me to take a back seat as my mother declined.

Three weeks later, when my manager, who rarely communicated with me, sent me a meeting request at 5 p.m. on a Friday for 8 a.m. on Monday, I was prepared. I got laid off from the company where I had worked for 15 years … for the third time. That's right—not once, twice, but three times. Never for performance, always for role elimination, and coincidentally, all after I had kids. The first two times, I respected my managers, and I desperately wanted to stay in the company I loved so much. By the third time, I finally got the message.

On the call, she asked me how my mother was doing. When I replied that she was at her end, my manager responded with, "That's what makes this so hard for me." You can imagine my internal eye-roll that my mother's impending death made it difficult for my manager to fire me. As I did in the taxicab back from the ER, I was determined to surrender to the suck in order to extract myself from reliving Groundhog Day. I could not control the company's action; I could only control my reaction. This time, I decided to walk into the fire and leave gracefully. I replied to her,

"Fortunately, I've just wrapped up the preparation for one of the product keynote sessions for next week's Sales Kick Off. My guess is that it will be one of the highest-rated sessions in its workstream." It was.

Let me be clear, my experience is not an indictment of Cisco Systems. These things happen at large companies. Even upon departure, I was grateful to a company that offered me breadth and depth in technology. However, I do question if a white man of talent would have been laid off three times—never for performance, always for role elimination, and only after he had kids. Coincidence? Or unconscious bias?

When I took the time to *reflect,* I had to admit that despite continuing to receive profuse accolades and impressive awards, the reality was that my career had been falling off a cliff for 10 years. Not only did I struggle to move up, I was finding myself increasingly at risk in an increasingly toxic work environment. Although I was still confident in my competence, each layoff took a bite out of my ego.

With nowhere to go, I had to *recalibrate.* I had reason after reason to stay in the status quo. But at the end of the day, when limiting reasons are stripped away, all that lays bare are fear and naked excuses. Leaving would force me to take a leap of faith and stare down the paralysis that had been preventing me from making a change. I thought about consulting for years, but never had the guts to start my own business. With a generous severance package and the Affordable Care Act, I now had some leeway.

It was time to *reset.* It is easy to think of the end of a long-term relationship, whether it's with a person or a company, as a personal failure. There are feelings of abandonment, betrayal, and guilt. Look for the gift embedded in necessary losses. Grief is learning to survive the letting go of something you desperately want to keep—sometimes by choice, but more often, not. It could be the mourning of status quo, a life experience, a person, or a career. Grief has shaped me first as a human, then as a professional, then as a leader.

There is nothing that accelerates self-growth faster than recovering from pain. As disaster after disaster struck in the seven years between the deaths of my parents, there were days I couldn't get out of bed, thinking, "Why does life hate me?" But with each difficulty, I became more grounded in my purpose and my recovery accelerated. After my father's death, leaving my perfect life in Austin took three months and turning the page on my marriage took three years. In contrast, after my mother's death, my decision to leave my company took three days. With each painful event, I was quicker to distinguish learning opportunities from toxicity. Each time, I became less fearful about surrendering to the suck to face the decisions I had been ignoring, but were necessary for my growth.

I'm reminded of a tale about a hurricane in Louisiana. As the waters were rising, everyone was instructed to evacuate. One man refused to leave.

An emergency vehicle came by and called for the man to evacuate. He refused. "God will save me," he declared.

As the water rose, his neighbor came by with a boat and offered him a ride out. The man refused again. "God will save me," he pronounced.

Day turned to night and the water levels grew higher. The man was on his roof when a helicopter came by and dropped a ladder. The man still refused, "God will save me."

Sadly, he drowned in the flood. In the afterlife, the man asked God, "I had faith. Why didn't you save me?" God looked down at the man and said, "I sent you a van, a boat, and a helicopter. What more did you want from me?"

Reflecting on the waters of marginalization that rose around me, I realize now that each difficulty was a gift I failed to recognize. Losing my father gave me the permission to embrace the audacity of my ambition and to move to California. Losing my job the first time and acknowledging my loneliness in the taxi to the ER gave me the courage to face the end of my marriage and to move to the Bay Area. Losing my job a second time forced me to make the leap into sales that I had always been too practical to pursue. And finally, losing my mother at the same time I was being ejected from my company for the third time gave me the courage to admit that staying on course was causing me to spiral out of control. I let go of the comfort of a status quo that was no longer serving me. It prompted me to leave a company that had been my security blanket for 15 years. Accepting these challenges meant accepting reality, accepting myself, and accepting accountability to pave my own path.

How do you know when it's time to let go? What do you take ownership of, and what should you walk away from? It is often repeated, "People leave managers, not companies." In 2015, Gallup reported that 50 percent of US workers "left their job to get away from their manager," and less than one-third of Americans are engaged in their jobs, a statistic that has remained consistent for over 15 years. Here are some questions I worked through during my time of healing and reflection:

- Does your company promote good leaders or political players?
- Do your leaders model integrity and excellence?
- Is your team a collaborative work family, or are you fighting for survival à la *Lord of the Flies*?
- How does your organization react to inappropriate behavior? Do they come down on those in power, or do they coach those in the minority to sit down and shut up?
- The most important introspection on deciding to depart: Has your own behavior become toxic? If so, either get it together or get out before you contaminate others.

Grief demands unconstrained vulnerability. Healing demands unconstrained courage to surrender to the suck. If you try to avoid it and kick the can down the road, you may lose a precious opportunity to discover a piece of your soul you didn't even know you were missing. Transcending grief requires facing the person in the mirror, what they stand for, and what they believe. Rebirth requires fully accepting the problem in order to find your way out of it. Go ahead and face the drama of the trauma head on. If you find the grit to survive it, only then can the phoenix emerge from the fire.

Fine. I could do this. I had spent my entire life finding ways to thrive amidst obstacles of adversity. My family defied insurmountable odds to immigrate to the United States with nothing but the clothes on our backs the day before Saigon fell. Despite growing up as an outsider in poverty, I excelled academically, professionally, and personally. Because that's what tenacious immigrants do.

By the time the shit hit the fan between 2007 and 2014, I survived the deaths of two parents, a cross-country move, an egregious lawsuit, a landslide, a home burglary, a divorce, and three layoffs. Yup. I'm a survivor. I could do this. I was determined to stop *denying* my destiny and start *designing* my destiny so I could thrive again. This would be the beginning of my professional metamorphosis.

Control what you can, influence what you can't, and recognize when to let go of good to make room for great. Just as Andra Day sings, "*Rise up* and do it a thousand times again."

Chapter 9
Pick Your Poison

"If you just set out to be liked,
you will be prepared to compromise on anything at any time,
and would achieve nothing."

– Margaret Thatcher

A story about women in the workplace would be incomplete without an open discussion about perfectionism and self-care, or lack thereof. As a woman, a very real struggle exists between home and career. As an immigrant, a very real struggle exists between honoring your culture and seeking your fulfillment. There are so many factors in the decision-making behind disrupting your relationships or pursuing your ambitions. What will your family think? What will your friends think? How will they react? For the longest time, I was paralyzed by all these outside factors. "I'm not going to take a leap of faith right now because I don't want to damage my family, my team or this, that, or the other."

I've been accused of being fervently, and sometimes overwhelmingly, authentic. It's because I've suffered the emotional and physical pain of being disingenuous. In 2008, my body shut down from living a life that was prescribed for me, but not defined by me. As I was going through my divorce and bouts of gastrointestinal pain, I had to take ownership of my compliance in letting others and myself box me in.

It is not unusual for working mothers to also remain primary caregivers. Let me tell you, it is not sustainable—you CANNOT have it all, and definitely not at the same time. You can accelerate certain aspects of your life at certain times with intentional trade-offs in other areas. Most importantly, you CANNOT do it all alone. Otherwise, the cocktail you may find in your hand in the wee hours of the morning will be Lidocaine with a Maalox chaser.

Having grown up in the "and" culture, I've always wanted to be a mother *and* a career woman. But I've never wanted to bake cookies for all the teachers and students, nor did I want to be a CEO of a Fortune 100 company. As you can see in my 2002 life plan, it took me a very long time to understand that I had choices in between. I didn't want to pick sides, so I didn't. What I underestimated was the amount of internal and external pressures to lose myself in either my family or my career.

When we first moved to the San Diego area, my son was five years old and my daughter was three years old. I knew I uprooted my family from Texas for my own happiness and career, so I was going to make it up to them by being an even better homemaker. Still married but working from home with the kids, I woke up at 5:00 a.m. in the morning to make homemade French toast with freshly whipped cream, topped with strawberries. I got them to school by 7 a.m. and worked till 3 p.m., at which time I would shuttle them off to various afterschool activities until my husband could take over when he came home from work. After making dinner and sending everyone to bed, I would turn my laptop back on around 11 p.m. for a couple hours of work before catching a few hours of sleep. 5.00 a.m. alarm. Wash. Rinse. Repeat. On weekends, I learned to make Coq Au Vin, Osso Buco, and Moroccan Tagine. And let's throw in key lime pie for good measure. As you may recall, this was also while I was trying to redeem myself from layoff #1.

Why do we do this to ourselves? Who put this gun to our heads? If we haven't yet found the courage to take our expectations off road, we're stuck trying to comply with cultural and societal definitions of a good daughter, wife, and mother. Just as it's important to label our values, it's important to name our pain. Naming provides an acknowledgement that moves the pain from the emotional amygdala to the logical frontal cortex. It makes it tangible, so we can recognize it and take ownership of our choices. Anyone can offer us different kinds of poison, but we alone have the choice to drink from the vial. Let's see what various yummy cocktails we can make with the ingredients in our cupboards.

Poison #1: Perfectionism. As women, we internalize societal expectations to take care of everyone else before ourselves. Referring back to Maslow's hierarchy, if women are supposed to support our male partners' careers while we shore up the household, ambitious women *still* generally take on the primary responsibility of ensuring that our house is a home. So, we end up striving to do both. Perfectly. Too perfectly. To the point of manic control. Sometimes, we even chastise our husbands for not doing their household chores correctly. Then we grumpily take over anyway when he offers to help. Have I mentioned that in trying to keep my family together, I wasn't a particularly pleasant partner?

At work, how much of the "office housework" do we take on? How often do we personally execute on tasks that can be delegated? How many women buy the birthday cake for the office mate, then volunteer to cut it for everyone in the breakroom? I'm not saying everyone should throw their hands up and look out for #1. I'm saying look around to see if everyone is rolling up their sleeves, as well. Remember that your insistence on being meticulous can be used against you. Before laptops followed us into conference rooms, I remember always being asked to take notes because I had better handwriting. I remember always being the person to document the project plan because I was "the most organized." If you're always the person doing the doing, you lose opportunities to be the person doing the thinking.

Poison #2: Gender roles. Societal expectations are real. What does it mean to be a good woman? In what context do we compare ourselves? Of course, no story will be 100 percent the same for everyone, but there is a general assumption of everlasting marriage and motherhood. I'm going to be provocative in saying that, in America, the ability to have one parent stay at home is an unrecognized privilege. In affluent circles, it has almost become an expectation, which also generally lands on the shoulders of women. It is absolutely a respectable choice to follow that model, but what if a couple doesn't want children? If they do, what if neither parent wants to stay at home full-time? What if both want to be involved with the children? If you look at how private schools and public schools in wealthy zip codes are structured, there is a high dependence on parental engagement.

It is incredibly frustrating when meetings among parents are scheduled in the middle of the day. It's insulting when administrators, teachers, and coaches address mothers when asking for volunteers and look at fathers when asking for money. Some ideas are a smart investment into the child's development, while other initiatives are just absolutely ridiculous. I don't know how many emails I've received guilting parents into "the lunch line cannot survive without parent volunteers," or something similar. Last year, I read a neighborhood call to action for parents to monitor every road corner for a half mile around the school during commute hours so our children would feel safe to bike and walk to school. Seriously, who has time for that? Why don't we just strip our kids of all resilience and bubble wrap them instead?

This same definition of a good daughter, wife or mother doesn't necessarily translate to immigrants. In the Vietnamese experience, everyone—father, mother, children—financially contributes to the family. However, her husband's needs and career always take priority, followed by her family's needs, then her own. I have plenty of immigrant girlfriends who earn more income than their husbands, but he's still the decision maker in the household. On the other hand, if her husband is a multi-millionaire, she still feels compelled to make her own money as part of her self-worth. Even when the couple's finances are commingled, being a good wife for many immigrant women includes being self-sufficient *and* being the primary caregiver.

So, I'm curious, in what context do *you* define a good woman? From what social narrative are you drawing your belief system? Which of these is right? Which is wrong? I would argue none and all. Try to consider the definitions for yourself, without prejudice. And here's the important part—know that this definition is personal to you. Don't impose *your* definition on another woman. Unintentionally, this is how women end up looking down our noses as we serve poison to each other.

This shows up at work as the Motherhood Penalty, a term used by sociologists to describe systematic disadvantages that working mothers encounter relative to childless women in hiring practices, wages, perception, and promotion penalties. The pay gap between non-mothers and mothers is actually larger than the gap between men and women. The widening disparity between male/female ratios higher up the career ladder is often explained by a leaky pipeline of women opting out of the workplace when they have children. Mothers are often perceived to be less dependable and less committed to their jobs than women without children.

When mothers exit the corporate world, do we ask why, or do we make assumptions? Certainly, many couples prefer to have one parent stay home with the children. But does it always have to be the mother? And does it have to be forever? Do we really believe that all women are better parents than all men, at all times? Why isn't there a fatherhood penalty? As a young mother, if I had to leave early to pick up the children, I was seen as distracted from work, as a matter of course. If my male colleague did the same, he was seen as a hero for "stepping up" out of his role.

I could have easily become part of the leaky pipeline statistic. I didn't start my own business because I wanted more temporal flexibility for childcare. I didn't leave corporate because the work required to climb was too hard. I left corporate because navigating the politics of an inaccurate perception of working mothers was too difficult. I had an argument with a man I was dating who was baffled when I said I would have much preferred to be the parent who had the privilege of working until 7 p.m. every night instead of being the primary parent on duty. He didn't believe me. That relationship didn't last.

Poison #3: Immigrant guilt. As immigrants, we come to the United States with a fire and desire. Contrary to divisive messaging, immigrants arrive with hope for a hand up, not with expectations for a handout. We're willing to work. Many of us come from cultures that value the health of the community over the individual. The primary duty of the younger generation is to take care of our parents, grandparents, aunts, uncles, nieces, nephews, cousins, in-laws ... and the guy on the street that did something nice for one of us 14 years ago. Between the gratitude for having the opportunity to rise and the overwhelming responsibility for generosity ingrained in our culture, it's exhausting.

Again, let's be *real* real. Of course, our parents want us to be successful, but part of the reason we're bullied into certain careers is for the pure vanity of bragging rights within the community. "See how smart my kid is? See how practical and obedient they are?" There are financial considerations, as well. Because pensions and 401ks are American concepts, most immigrants don't have similar retirement funds. For this reason, the older generation also relies on the next generation for support throughout their later years. So, they want us to make a safe choice. Doctor, lawyer, engineer—pick one. Or in the case of a young woman, pharmacist or accountant, please.

Like my siblings, I contributed to the family as early as I could. I started working at a formalwear store, counting inventory after hours at the age of 14 and put myself through university with scholarships, aid, and working 20 hours a week on top of a full load of classes. When I received my first professional check from AMD at 19, I immediately began sending monthly checks to my mother, a story she would continue to tell her friends proudly, even in her final years. Because that's the responsibility immigrants carry.

We're also highly discouraged from moving out of town to ensure not only the emotional closeness of the family, but the physical proximity of future grandbabies that may be five to ten years in the making. As each child moved out of state to escape our toxic household, my dad's sadness increased. He complained that his friends' children stayed in town at the small expense of letting go of higher potential careers outside of Baton Rouge. I'm sure I saw his heart break a little in front of me when I told him I was foregoing the full ride to Louisiana State University to pursue engineering at the University of Texas in Austin. As immigrants, we are constantly torn between seeking validation from our parents, while pursuing a definition of fulfillment they don't understand.

When immigrants struggle, we compare our journeys to those of our ancestors. It's a sobering reality check. Nothing we face can be nearly as difficult as what they survived. This is the immigrant version of "my grandparents walked five miles to school barefoot in the snow, uphill in both directions," which is basically "It could always be worse." Dude, it's not a competition to the bottom. That's not how to measure a life.

This rationalization sets a pretty low bar for happiness. Society expects that women will only leave a marriage in the case of infidelity or physical abuse. What if your path has simply diverged, draining all intimacy and connection in your relationship? What if you know it's not right because it no longer *feels* right? Your amygdala can sense the unhappiness. And guess what—your kids can, too. I no longer prescribe to, "I should stay if my man isn't beating on me." Come on, sisters. What kind of a bar is that?

The same is true at work. I often tell people that of my 15 years at Cisco, I stayed seven years too long. My loyalty and guilt paralyzed me from walking away when my growth was stunted. In my career, I no longer prescribe to, "I should stay as long as I'm earning a decent paycheck," regardless of getting randomly moved around with no choice, no voice, and no promotion. Personally and professionally, when I'm on a broken conveyor belt now, I step off of it and keep walking. Even if your feet are glued down by the sticky tar of guilt, get yourself unstuck. No one's gonna do it for you. Step off the belt anyway.

Just because someone's life has been harder than yours, doesn't diminish the pain in your own journey. My mother once said to me, "nhìn xuống thì không ai bằng, nhìn lên thì không bằng ai," which means, "looking down, no one is your equal, looking above, you are equal to no one."

Poison #4: Unworthiness. Multigenerational Americans may contrast their lives to those of people in second and third world countries, in gratitude for their blessings. Immigrants contrast their lives to the hardship of their parents' or ancestors' journeys. Either way, you wake up every day with the perspective to move beyond your struggles.

Here's the negative effect we don't talk about. Immigrant parents? They play on that pressure. They don't mean to, but they instill guilt in you. They will imbue in conversations the sacrifices they made to give you opportunities you're flagrantly throwing away. It's not like you need the daily reminder of what they went through to take full advantage of the access they never had. But they're going to remind you anyway. I should know, I did it to my kids until I went into the ER. On one hand, children of immigrants are taught to be grateful for what they have while never being satisfied with what they give. They are never good enough. Nothing they do can live up to the sacrifices made for them. These self-limiting beliefs are the curse of adversity. On one side of the coin is tenacity, on the other side is self-imposed pressure.

I remember watching a YouTube video in 2005, called *Crazy Asian Mother*, by Erick Liang. He shows his grades to his mother, knowing he was going to be in a lot of trouble for getting an "Asian F," more widely known in our community as a B+. In the video, his mother says,

Let's see what you got in all your classes.
Physics: A
US History: A
AP Calculus: A ...
Chemistry: A. That's good, that's real good ...
Programming: A ...
Spanish: A
What? B+ in English? [mother hyperventilates]
Eric Tsai - how did you get a B+ in English, huh?
We come all the way, from that far country, China, and we born you here in America, just so you can get B+? That unacceptable.
Tell me why! Why did you get a B+ in English?

This video was so funny because it was so true. I remember my father displaying our report cards on the refrigerator. In red marker, he circled the one B+ among all the A's. That silent red circle shamed us much more loudly than harsh words ever could. Pair this unworthiness with perfectionism, and between work and home, you can easily earn yourself a trip to the emergency room.

Poison #5: Self-sacrifice. The fact that your parents survived horrific odds may motivate you to overcome any barriers you may face. But wait a minute. Don't forget that everyone deserves their own definition of happiness. Do you want to just survive, or do you want to thrive? The downside of this tenacity is running yourself into the ground while taking care of everyone else's well-being and expectations. It's like my dad not cashing the damn checks to pay for his medication. It's like me, waking up to make French toast at 5 a.m. every damn day until I landed in the hospital. Who asked me to? Who expected me to?

When you're running around taking care of everyone else, consider what it is that you're doing for yourself. Are you getting joy toiling away?

Are you truly giving, or are you practicing the selfish act of alleviating guilt from old narratives? Do people really even need the level of care you're providing? Of course, my kids appreciated French toast at 5 a.m., but they didn't need it every day. With full context, they would have much preferred having more cereal in exchange for their mother's serenity.

A Cocktail to Die For

Now let's mix a shot of a woman's perfectionism with a shot of immigrant guilt. Shake it up. Stir in the social expectations of Maslow's hierarchy of needs. Then top it with a cherry of unworthiness. There's no room for your own happiness in that drink. How about another cocktail of gender roles with a splash of self-sacrifice? Mmm ... irresistible. You know what? Who needs a complicated cocktail when you can take straight shots? A little bit of this one and a little bit of that one. How much poison will you voluntarily ingest over time? It can happen so gradually that the deterioration is unnoticeable. Just as drinking alcohol alone is a sure sign of alcoholism, continuously taking poison in the corner of a lonely mental box is a sure sign of martyrdom.

Does this analogy seem dark to you? That's because it is. Don't shift your mindset *as if* your life depends on it. Shift your mindset *because* your life depends on it. Train yourself to get out of the abyss by surrendering to the suck, picking up the can, and dealing with your shit. It is much more tempting to stay in your comfort zone, letting yourself get pulled back into self-sacrificing in the name of others. Just one more slice of toast. Just one more drive to another after-school activity. Just one more month, one more year, one more benchmark before I work on myself or my career. Just one more distraction that I can use as an excuse to kick the can down the road.

It took the death of one parent for me to notice these habits, and the death of a second parent before I addressed it. While death of a loved one provides perspective for what's really important, waiting for someone you love to die to give you an epiphany is not a path I recommend for anyone. When my father left this world, it wasn't as if my brain clicked that same day, "Now I'm going to think differently." It doesn't work that way. It would take three years of soul searching and a bunch of other crap to happen in the interim. There was a long transition from the initial acknowledgement that despite my storybook life, I felt like the biggest loser. Then came the acceptance that I was forcing myself to be happy about being *not un*happy. And finally, came the realization that it doesn't matter what it looks like to the outside world. if you're dying inside, you're dying inside. Full stop.

Reflect. Think of your life in chapters, without shame. You may find both ends of each of the career and caregiver spectrums appealing at some level at any time. That's the point. You don't have to limit yourself to binary gender specific roles, and if you do, it doesn't have to be forever. You have the right to evolve. Depending on where you are in your life, your priorities may change, indefinitely, or not.

Recalibrate. If you're intentional and you're fortunate to have a willing partner on the same page, the two of you will be able to disaggregate Maslow's hierarchy from traditional male/female roles. You can choose who will be in the career spotlight, and for how long. You can choose who will be the sparkle in your children's eyes, and for how long. If both partners decide to play both parts, you can continuously and lovingly modulate the brightness of each light. And if you can't, dare I say it? Your life partner may or may not be by your side in the same capacity for the full journey. It's okay for both of you to turn the page. Together. Compassionately.

Reset. Think of your relationship in the context of content, not form. The love that my ex-husband and I shared as a couple for 16 years has continued to live on for the next 10 years. The content of respect, support, and affection is the same, only the form has changed. Although we no longer share an address, we are still committed to our children and our lifelong friendship. In trying to artificially stay together, as the form stopped working, the content of our relationship began falling apart. In the case of our divorce, just because the form changed, it didn't mean the content had to sour. My story is living proof that it is possible to transition from loving spouses to loving co-parents who support each other from afar.

Think of your career as a journey, not a single destination. If you're intentional and fortunate to work for a company that allows you to disaggregate Maslow's hierarchy from traditional male/female roles, you can maximize your professional potential. And if you can't, dare I say it? There might not be a cultural fit. It's okay for you and the company to turn the page. Be open to letting your career unfold, wherever it may lead.

In my personal and professional life, I had to remind myself to "keep fighting voices in my mind that say I'm not enough, every single lie that tells me I will never measure up," as Lauren Daigle sings in *You Say*.

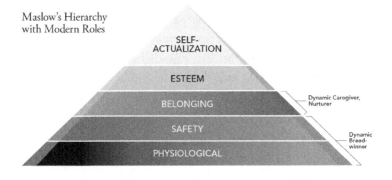

Chapter 10
The Road to Recovery

"When we deny our history and pain, our history and pain own us. When we have the courage to own our stories of pain, fear, and oppression, we can write a new story."

– Brené Brown

If my experience has taught me anything, it's that you can't really succeed professionally until you take care of yourself personally. In my last two weeks at Cisco Systems, I went to my doctor for a regular exam. This time, my emotional distress manifested into physical symptoms of insomnia and a familiar digestive pain. She coaxed me into sharing my story. Reluctantly, I admitted to being disillusioned and disoriented. As a high achiever, how did I get here? A laid off single mother of two young children, living in a two-bedroom apartment the size of a postage stamp. My doctor promptly shared her own story. She got divorced in her early 40s, started medical school, and rebuilt her family. I was in awe. Can you really reboot your life? When she mandated that I go on medical leave, I protested fiercely. That's when she directly addressed my Achilles' heel, the need to take care of the people important to me. She mentally shook me, "You cannot show up as the best person, parent, and professional until you show up for yourself."

Self-Compassion

For years, I knew at my core that my career and marriage were over in their current forms, I just didn't have the tools to uncover it. I lacked the skills to process my feelings, yet I rejected the concept of psychotherapy. Having always been the black sheep in the bunch, I was uncomfortable reaching out to my family and friends, even though I knew how much they cared about me. I didn't want to face the shame of failure. In isolation and without any support, I tried to deal with it on my own and fell into a lonely, debilitating depression.

When you're under stress, take care of your basic needs. Eat. Sleep. Move your body to get the endorphins flowing. It's never too late. I only started running and lifting regularly in my late 30s. Treat yourself with the compassion you would show for a close friend—not your partner (you're probably harsher with them then most) but think of the generosity and patience you would provide to a friend. And for everyone's sake, get out of bed and take a shower. It's hard, I know. Do it, anyway.

When you're under duress, swallow your pride and get the help you need. Open up to your friends and family. But if you smell drama, give yourself the space to step away from the toxicity of those who would judge you harshly. When those close to me chastised me for not leaning on them during my time of need, I asked them, "How have you supported me before? What would you have said to me this time? Would you have been able to listen without judgement? Or would you immediately launch into giving me advice without context?" Because I've not been one to conform, I didn't need the stress of validation for getting what I deserved for being unconventional. In my mind, I'm screaming Mother Teresa's words at them, "If you judge people, you have no time to love them."

If you don't feel supported in your immediate network, open it up. Find support groups or confide in people who have had similar experiences. You may be surprised to find compassion where you least expect it. If you're lucky, you may find someone who truly sees you—someone who really gets you and can help you find the clarity you need to surrender to the suck and embrace your courage. They are there to witness your journey and provide the compassion you can't find for yourself. Having someone completely and selfishly invested in you gives you the permission to validate your experience, from mere machinations of your mind to facts of worthy substance. If they challenge you to face the uncomfortable, hold on tight. These true friends are few and far between. It is a gift to have someone hold up a mirror for you. Don't push them away. Just as windows of opportunities close, friends can only be dismissed for so long before they disappear, as well. Embrace their edge so you can find your own.

If none of the above works, brush away your preconceived aversions to getting outside help. Why wait for the death of a parent or a trip to the ER before seeking a therapist? What's the harm? What are they going to do? Kill you with conversation? Let's work through some of the mental barriers:

Protest: "I don't believe in therapy; they're all quacks."
Answer: "Do you read leadership books for tips and tricks of the trade? Would you accept executive coaching to get to the next step in your career? Do you know everything there is to know about neuroplasticity? How is opening your mind to therapy any different?"

Protest: "Fine. But it's probably hard to find a good therapist."
Answer: "It is. Anything worth it requires work."

Protest: "I can do it on my own."
Answer: "No. You can't. And even if you could, why take the hard road up the mountain when you can learn from lessons of previous treks?"

In both cases of my depression, my medical doctors insisted that I couldn't fix my body until I fixed my mind. Without help, I would not have learned about all the brain wiring working against me: the psychological concepts of the status quo bias, loss aversion, and the sunk cost fallacy. The brain defaults to mourning retrospectively, rather than rejoicing in possibilities proactively. In my depression, I was alternating between two treacherous paths: ruminating on sad thoughts, or worse, escaping into useless avoidance. Unbeknownst to me, doing either was making me susceptible to permanently rewiring my brain to a lower happiness setpoint. Your brain gets tired, so it gives up. It accepts sadness as normalcy. It resigns to a constant state of fearfulness. And worse of all, it lets you wallow in selfish victimhood. That is not the human I chose to be. So, I got help.

When I was in one of my deepest troughs, my therapist conducted a ground-breaking exercise with me. She asked me to give her my personal statement of purpose in one sentence. She scribbled with an orange dry-erase marker on the whiteboard adjacent to her desk. I uttered from the couch, "I need to be the best at everything that I do." She capped the marker, and said, "That's a lot of pressure. No wonder you've been in therapy for years." I laughed out loud and said, "I actually cut off the last part of the sentence, 'all the time.'"

We spent the next hour and a half breaking down every single word and figuring out where it came from: my childhood, my culture, my experience, etc. From there, she helped me develop a new statement of purpose. With a red marker, she would strike out one word at a time, and we would replace it with another word in black or green marker. With each word exchange, I could feel my body relax. We softened the original statement to read, "I want to learn from each of my experiences as best as I can." And in lieu of, "all the time," we appended, "as much as possible."

Part of the transactional analysis we discussed in "Sit Down and Shut Up" is about the drivers in our communication paths. Somewhere in our Parent-Child memory recordings are beliefs that we have mapped in our heads, "I'm not good enough," or, "I'm only good enough if... " In order to begin truly accepting ourselves, we have to change that narrative. It's that simple. Yet simple is hard. Think about *your* value statement. Where does each word come from, and how can you be kinder to yourself?

In an executive coaching session, I learned about a psychological limiting belief change technique. Think of something that you know to be true, such as, "I know I am a woman" or "somewhere in the world the sun is rising." Map these indisputable facts with "empowering beliefs," such as, "I'm good enough as I am." Because we know the former to be true, we associate that known truth to a truth we want to establish, that we are indeed, good enough.

Let's neutralize those poisons with this technique, shall we?

- *Poison #1: Perfectionism. Truth* = The world is constantly changing. *Association* = You have permission to evolve and grow.
- *Poison #2: Gender roles. Truth* = You are human. *Association* = You are not limited to binary options of career or family.
- *Poison #3: Immigrant guilt. Truth* = You are a product of strength. *Association* = You are allowed to take care of yourself and welcome help when it is offered.
- *Poison #4: Unworthiness. Truth* = The sun comes up every day. *Association* = You are good enough. Just for good measure, let's repeat this one again. You. Are. Good. Enough.
- *Poison #5: Self-sacrifice. Truth* = In an emergency, you need to put your oxygen mask on first, before tending to the people in your care. *Association* = Mere survival is NOT the destination, and joy is NOT a luxury.

The vast majority of people tolerate these different poisons because they don't recognize the many forms that bullying and abuse can take. It is painful to admit that, regardless of intent, unwelcome coercion from "ordained authority" amounts to bullying. Stonewalling by a loved one on personal growth is a form of control. The cognitive dissonance we are unwilling to accept is that often, our abusers are the people who love us the most and who we love the most.

Our bodies tell us when something is wrong. Little by little, we experience death by a thousand paper cuts. In my case, poison accumulated until it could no longer be ignored. From *The Body Keeps the Score* by Bessel van der Kolk, "Erasing awareness and cultivating denial are often essential to survival, but the price is that you lose track of who you are, of what you are feeling, and of what and who you can trust." The book discusses that when abuse is disclosed, the perpetrator reacts with violent betrayal and hurt. The fear of this reaction causes the abused to keep protecting their abuser by hiding and denying it, deflecting blame to something external, such as frivolity, a mid-life crisis, or even a global pandemic, which only compounds the shame and guilt.

Think about when you feel particularly well, or not.

- Who are you with, and what are you doing in each case?
- How do you feel when you wake up in the morning? Are you energized, or are you merely surviving by emptily going through the motions for the day, week, or month?
- Apply this to any relationship. Are you excited to wake up to the human next to you? Are you excited to go to work? Does the stress of one give you the excuse not to deal with the other?

It's not just women. Men also struggle with societal and cultural definitions of a good son, husband, and father. Some want to step back on their career. Some want to close the chapter on a marriage. Men, women, we're all more similar than we are different; our struggles are simply different sides of the same coin. I've had the same exchange so many times with numerous male and female friends:

Friend: "I don't know what's wrong with me. My life is so much better than most. I should be happy that I'm *not un*happy."
Me: "Sounds familiar. Everyone deserves their own definition of happiness. It is unfair to use other people's suffering as an excuse. What does your family think? How are they supporting you?"

Friend: "I don't want to burden them with my frivolity."
Me: "Your pain is not frivolous. Your family loves you. Allow them to be part of the conversation so they can help you."

Friend: "No one can help me."
Me: "The adults in the equation have the right to know your truth so they can react with their truth. You're taking their choice away from them."

Friend: "My dreams are unrealistic."
Me: "Maybe. Maybe not. How do you know? If you could wave a magic wand, what would your life look like?"

Friend: "It would look like X-Y-Z, which would require some major, impossible changes."
Me: "Anything is possible. Who or what is holding you back? What are you losing by self-selecting out?"

Friend: "I can't do this to my family or my team."
Me: "Don't they deserve to know who you really are? What do you want to model for them? A brave, authentic human, or the shell of one?"

Only then does the real introspection start. After this exchange, one of my close friends expressed his concerns to me, "my brain is messing with my body." Almost a decade after my ER experience, I told him, "No, your body is telling you something your brain refuses to accept." Consider for yourself, what issues do you need to face? You have to choose if you're going to live for your own happiness or die slowly day after long day on the gray grindstone.

Reflect. At the end of the day, we want to do the right thing. But how much of that desire is driven by *looking* like we're doing the right thing in order to ensure a positive social perception? As my dad was dying with all his regrets, he realized—who cares? Who do you serve when you suffer? Personally, it took a cross-country move and two trips to the ER for me to face the fact that my career was stunted and my marriage had been over for years. All that was left were smoke and mirrors. Professionally, I had to be pushed off the cliff's edge three times before I was willing to hear the call to my hero's journey. Think of who or what is holding you back. A good measure is if people you love openly know who and what you love deeply. Do they really see you as you are today? Or do they only see the child you once were or the young professional they first met?

Ask yourself the following:

- Whose acceptance am I seeking? What "ordained authority" makes their opinion law?
- What potential beauty am I letting go of by refusing to take my expectations off road?
- Who is being cruel to me by holding me back, and who am I being cruel to by my inability to act and blossom?

Recalibrate. It is okay to accept yourself as you are today and to accept the dreams you have for tomorrow. You are worthy of happiness. I recall a conversation with a dear friend, as I was trying to talk myself out of taking action. I simply said, "The grass isn't always greener on the other side," to which she quickly responded, "Darlin', sometimes when you're standing in a patch of brown grass, it's a patch of brown grass."

Feed your needs so you have the energy to feed those around you. Once you invest in yourself, the fog will lift, and you will begin to gain clarity. Shed the expectations around you and accept your authentic self. As Dr. Seuss once said, "Those who mind don't matter, and those who matter don't mind." Who loves you for who you truly are versus who you're pretending to be? Here are some of my key takeaways from Brené Brown's special on Netflix, *The Call to Courage*:

- True connection is a result of authenticity.
- Blame is a way to discharge pain and discomfort, so it is unnecessary to blame yourself for a situation that is blameless— it just is.

- Children are wired for struggle—our job is not to keep their lives perfect.
- Let your vulnerability outsmart shame, giving yourself permission to experience true joy.

When my parents died, I decided to live. My threshold is no longer set at "stick around until things are unbearably shitty." I don't have that many fucks to give anymore, so I've learned to budget them well. Not everyone and everything can be a priority. Frankly, when I accepted my own worthiness, I realized that not everyone or everything deserves my attention. When I hear someone telling me, "I don't have time" for something, I press further. Anyone has time for anything. In fact, one of my therapists shared with me, "If you want to get something done, give it to a busy person. They know how to juggle efficiently." The more honest answer is, "This is not a priority at the moment."

At home and work, control what you can, influence what you can't, and let go of good to make room for great. That means evaluating if your current situation is the right fit moving forward. Then go on a relationship diet. Invest in people who uplift you, versus those who hold you back from your true happiness. Avoid those who want to control you, and treasure those who empower you. At work, this means standing up for yourself. It's a rare bird that I am unable to collaborate with. I can almost always bring other people along by neutralizing their fear of differences with overwhelming compassion and information. The seven-year-old on the playground reminds me to "kill them with kindness and upper cut them with data." Occasionally, there is an immovable asshole. Smile and nod, then influence around them. If you're in a room full of immovable assholes, you're in a toxic environment. It's not you; it's them. Get the hell out.

Reset. It's okay to pursue self-actualization, even if it leads to non-ideal outcomes that expose you to judgment from others. There's nothing wrong with paving your own path. Before you can expect anyone else to release you from the stigma of being an ambitious woman, you have to release yourself from that belief first. Break free of those judgments and pursue your dreams without regrets. It's not instant. Allow yourself some space to wallow in victimhood for a moment, then give yourself a timeline of the steps you're going to take to snap out of it. Taking a breath is surviving. Hiding under a rock is just hiding.

How do you want to live? You have a choice between paralysis or progress.

- Look back on your history of happiness and unhappiness: what are the trends?
- Look forward to what you want in your next chapters, and when.
- Write your own narrative. What brings you joy, and who is there when you are most authentic?

The truth is that you DO have a magic wand. It is within you. The stem of the wand is made of courage and authenticity; the sparkly tip is made of deliberate intention.

According to former speech writer for Vice President Al Gore and author on business and behavior, Daniel Pink notes in his MasterClass that we think "our beliefs shape our actions, but our actions can shape our beliefs." Be willing to be dynamic. Sometimes it's just about building momentum. How are you being challenged to think differently? What small steps can you take to create some momentum? In Daniel Pink's words:

- Use this moment of awareness as an alarm clock rather than a snooze button.
- Give yourself interim goals.
- Make a public commitment to someone to keep yourself accountable.

Through my trials, I have learned to unapologetically respect myself by honoring my needs. I celebrate my gifts and give myself permission to completely suck at certain things, like group sports and baking. I'm determined to stop drinking random poison served to me, and to do my best to offer the same acceptance of each person's unique path. I seek environments where I will thrive by gravitating to those who would support me, rather than judge me. I've designed my life around authenticity to bring my whole, best self to the table, so that I am not susceptible to being abused or becoming the abuser. In doing so, I hope to encourage the most authentic, best self to emerge out of others, as well.

Healing begins with accepting ourselves and each other, not despite our broken wings, but because of them. As Jacquie Lee belts out in the *Broken Ones*, "Just remember that we've all been broken once! Let's love the broken ones."

Chapter 11
Misfit to Maven

*"The struggles along the way are only meant
to shape you for your purpose."*

– Chadwick Boseman

My meritocratic upbringing left me completely unprepared later in my professional career. My peers were taking routes up the mountain that I couldn't even see with tools that weren't available to me. And dammit if I didn't stubbornly make it harder on myself by refusing to accept help along the way. We're taught to prepare for opportunities, but no one talks about preparing for the pitfalls when you reach the murky middle of your career.

Early on, there is much space for everyone at the base. The ascent begins with many, allowing special talent to emerge in proportion to an individual's skills. You get lulled into the myth of meritocracy. At some point, you hit a steep incline. Because intelligence and diligence has always worked, you expend tremendous energy and valuable time climbing with your bare hands, when you actually need grappling hooks. Better yet, you need someone to throw ropes down for you or show you the secret door to the secret tunnel. Unconscious bias is real, and lack of access is a massive roadblock. Without guidance, you need to find your own tools to get unstuck.

For years, I put immense pressure on myself to become a better professional by forcing myself to fit into a prescribed box of acceptability. I responded to feedback by pivoting my personal style so many times that I lost my identity. When I look back at the period between the three layoffs, I truly believe there was no malintent. I uncovered a huge perception problem. People in power could *look* at me as a doer, but they didn't have a lens with which to *see* me as a leader. They could *listen* to me, but they lacked the ability to *hear* me past their inherent judgements.

My eyes started opening to a truth I refused to believe for years. The rules of the game, the path up the mountain is different for me. In those years, we didn't have the vocabulary for unconscious bias. Although my mentors were well-intended, neither party realized that there were few people above me who looked like me or shared any semblance of my background. There were few women at the top and even fewer leaders who were women of color. After the second layoff, I appreciated that without leaders who look like me to clear the path, I would have to become my own guide and my own hero. *Of course,* prescribed formulas often did not apply to me, because they were never *written* by people like me. As a misfit, the gurus of corporate success had not walked in my shoes.

Representation matters. In an Instagram post celebrating Senator Kamala Harris as the first female of color to be nominated for the office of United States Vice President, I read,

> You get used to it, even as a little girl—opening the newspaper, turning on the TV, and hardly ever seeing anyone who looks like you. You train yourself to not get your hopes up. And sometimes it's a battle just to keep telling yourself that you might deserve more. Because no matter how much you prepare, no matter what grades you get or even how high you rise at work, it always feels like someone is waiting to tell you that you're not qualified. That you're not smart enough. That you're too loud or too bossy. That there's just something about you ... you're just not quite the right fit.

> - Michelle Obama, former First Lady

The same creativity sparked by my outsider's perspective was applauded in my work but frowned upon in perceptions of my edginess. Leaders loved the innovation in my output, but they were uncomfortable with the non-conformity in my thinking. It took three times for me to understand that I was no longer a cultural fit for my company. I think differently because I *am* different. That's the package, baby. You can't stand next to a spitfire in heels and complain about the heat.

As a woman, I was often measured by the length of my sleeve, rather than the height of my talent. There was more attention to the flashiness of my shoes than the creativity of my ideas. As a mother, I was held back for my potential lack of commitment, rather than awarded projects for which I raised my hand. As an immigrant and outsider, we already established that biology was conspiring against my trustworthiness and lack of access conspired against establishing my competence. As a remote worker, I was also judged by a misperception of low productivity, rather than recognized for the effective non-traditional hours I put in. During the COVID pandemic, it was amusing for me to watch the whole world realize that remote working was not only possible and highly productive, it led to employees burning out. I don't want to be one of those people who say, "I told you so" ... but ... "I told you so."

From years of trials and therapy, I learned to accept myself for being unapologetically ambitious and easily bored. I accepted my reality. I was misunderstood because I've been misrepresented by unconscious bias. Next, I had to accept my accountability. It was time to get out of my funk. It was time to release others' views of who I should be and the limits of what I could do. It was time to stop waiting for help to come in the form of leaders who could figure me out and magically appreciate me. It was time to reevaluate what I stood for, the woman I had become, and the woman I wanted to grow up to be. It was time to get unparalyzed, stop whining, and start doing. In a vacuum of leaders I could resonate with, I would have to become my own role model. The question is then, how do I go about transforming from misfit to maven without selling my soul?

After the second layoff, I was on a mission to re-establish myself. I read books, watched videos, attended various women's conferences, and took every workshop to heart. Two words kept coming up repeatedly: personal brand and network. Gross and double gross. I couldn't stand self-promotion, and I hated the inauthenticity of networking events. Even the word was unpalatable, "working the net." I wanted to change the rules. "Can't I just let my work speak for itself?" Umm ... apparently not. The spirit-of-Christmas-past Hang stepped into the room and smacked me upside the head, "Remember the layoffs? And the hospital? And the Lidocaine infused Maalox?" Oh. Right. Okay. Play the unfair game because you can't change the rules until you master it.

One day, Carla Harris threw me a lifeline from YouTube. I listened intently as the author of *Expect to Win* delivered her *Carla's Pearls of Wisdom* talk to an audience in Arizona. It was incomprehensible to me how this regal, intelligent, articulate Wall Street banker could have possibly struggled in her career. Yet she did. Then she figured out how to change the narrative around her, while remaining true to herself. When she talked about the power of authenticity, she said, "You are your own competitive advantage—nobody can be you the way that you can be you. The last thing that you should ever do is to submerge that which is uniquely you." She recalled a time when she had a 15-minute bonus meeting before the pitch meeting with a client because she "naturally differentiated herself" when "Carla Harris the singer was allowed to be in the room with Carla Harris the banker." And today, she brings all her Carlas to the table: the investment manager, the singer, the writer, the speaker, the football fan, because she doesn't know which one will connect to her audience. Okay, right on. Now we're getting somewhere.

Later, when she talked about perception being the co-pilot to reality, she finally bridged the gap for me between productivity and personality. "If you want to maximize your success in the seat that you're sitting in or the seat that you aspire to sit in, it is imperative that you understand the adjectives that are associated with success for the seat that you're sitting in or the seat that you aspire to sit in." She gave advice on how to train others to think about you. "Pick three adjectives that are consistent with who you really are ... however, pick three adjectives that are valued in that organization." Mind blown. This was advice that was applicable, actionable, *and* authentic.

When I coach my own team or groups of high potential talent, I ask them to do three things that I did for myself.

1. Define your values.
2. Understand your strengths.
3. Find your superpower.

Define your values. Taking Carla's advice to heart, I asked a handful of people I trusted—leaders, friends, family—to send three adjectives they would use to describe me. The nerd that I am put all these adjectives in a spreadsheet to find themes. I then focused on the ones that both resonated with me and would also be absolutely required in roles I aspired to. This exercise took a few months, but I concluded with curious, capable, and courageous—a mantra that has served me well since then.

To identify the essential qualities that will keep you grounded regardless of changing circumstances, follow this simple exercise:

- Make a list of 30 or so values. Narrow them down to 10 that resonate the most with you.
- Narrow those ten values again down to five.
- Make a list of values that are important to the role you want to succeed in.
- Match three adjectives that align with both your authentic self, as well as the company's needs.
- Exercise these three words consistently in your mindset, words, and actions.

Understand your strengths. After defining your values, understand how you can use your natural preferences to serve your purpose. Researcher and author of *StrengthsFinder 2.0*, Tom Rath, dissected decades of research by American psychologist, Don Clifton, to define strengths as follows:

Strengths = Talent x Investment.

Talent is defined as "naturally recurring patterns of thought, feeling, or behavior," while investment is "practice using them and adding knowledge and skills to them." Clifton took a maverick approach in studying success by posing the question, "What would happen if we studied what was right with people versus what's wrong with people?" We grow faster when we focus on developing areas of our greatest potential where we are innately gifted and energized, rather than trying to improve weaknesses that are awkward and frustrating.

After developing hundreds of predictive instruments that could identify top performers for organizations, his work led to the development of the *Clifton Strengths* assessment to benefit the individual. This is another powerful personal development tool that I use with my teams to understand our individual and collective strengths and blind spots, and how they distribute across the four domains of strategy, execution, relationship building, and influence. Gallup Research shows that people who have the opportunity to focus on their strengths every day are six times as likely to be engaged in their jobs and more than three times more likely to report having a better quality of life.

When I first tested as an individual contributor, my top five strengths were Activator, Relator, Strategic, Achiever, and Learner. Hmm ... so I'm good at motivating people to do impactful stuff by making it relatable with information. These top strengths shouldn't move much, with the exception of significant life experiences. After my trials and career ascension, I took the test again as an executive, and my top strengths were Activator, Maximizer, Significance, Analytical, and Command. So, I'm still good at making people do impactful stuff—I just make sure that we're doing the right things, and we're doing the right things right. And I'm unapologetically bossy about it. I'm an Asian Catholic mother raised in the Deep South. I do guilt, and I do bossy quite well. So how should I apply these strengths to work?

To unlock your potential,

- Invest in the short online Strengths test from Gallup. Identify talents that come naturally to you and skills that energize you when you practice and invest in improvement.
- Apply your strengths consistently to drive results.
- If a result requires a theme that is not one of your strengths, access another strength to achieve the same result. For instance, my low need for Context (understanding the present by considering the past) can be compensated by my Learner (learning for continuous improvement) attribute. My low Restorative (problem fixer) can be compensated by my Maximizer (stimulator of group excellence).

Find your superpower. Let's bring the prior two elements together to curate your authentic brand. Attach your strengths to the core values that inspire your internal decision making and external behaviors. What do you want to be known for as a human? As a professional? As a leader? Here are some things to think about as you rediscover yourself:

- What do you do?
- How do you do this?
- Why does what you do matter?
- What is the result of what you do?
- What are you known for?
- Who else does what you do?
- How are you different?
- What do you want to be remembered for?

Take these elements and develop your personal brand statement. Practice it as a ten-second pitch. Again. And again. Now develop your personal summary. Practice it as a two-minute pitch. Again. And again. It takes work. It takes time. Give it room to breathe and evolve. In ten seconds, I would describe my superpower as "the ability to inspire others to think or act differently by listening to them, understanding what drives them, and collaborating with them in a language they understand."

From this launch point, here's the two-minute pitch I've developed for myself over the past few years:

My professional and personal motivation: insatiable curiosity and an appetite for impact. I like doing big things, pushing boundaries, and executing on creative solutions to build flexible frameworks to scale the business. As an experienced leader in high-tech companies big and small, I'm constantly challenging my teams to see a broader picture by drawing upon my diverse background. Beyond race and gender, I bring perspectives from my depth of experience with complex problem solving in engineering, with product management and marketing, and from sales where I engage with customers and partners to communicate value in a way that motivates them to buy, instead of being sold to. We all have nicknames in our career, and I wear the name "Black Ops" with great pride. When faced with a challenge, I am known for proactively problem finding and strategically driving cutting edge solutions with surgical precision. With this mindset, my teams challenge the complacency of the status quo to uncover hidden opportunities and break down the elements that prevent us from being successful.

How about you? What's your personal pitch? While you're developing it, remember that fixing perception is not only about showing up, it's also about *how* you show up. Use the three R's to reflect on how can you personally *Earn it. Own it. Evolve it.* Develop an indisputable area of expertise and a reputation for collaboration and adaptability.

With branding, it's not only important to show what you *do*, it's important to de-emphasize what you *don't* do. I've had to train myself to stop being the mother hen. I've stopped offering to get coffee and water for everyone else in the room unless at least one other man is doing the same. Given that I'm usually surrounded by men, this should not be a tall order, but you'd be surprised. Put yourself in *their* shoes. What are the optics of finally having one woman enter the room, just for her to assign herself the task of taking care of everyone else's beverage needs? When I'm asked to do the office housework, I remind folks that I've already had a turn, and I insist on sharing the love. When it's pointed out that I'm just "better at it," I simply reply that I'm also good at cleaning but it's not where I want to spend all my time.

Catalytic Connections

Now that I figured out the brand thing authentically, how do I do the networking thing authentically? I got tired of waiting for luck and divine intervention, so I began creating my own conditions for the perfect storm. I'm sure you've heard, "It's not *what* you know. It's not *who* you know. It's *who* knows *what* you know." All right, how do I inform the rest of the world without feeling like I need to take a shower to wash the ick off? Practice with friendlies.

Realizing I had no network in the Bay Area and more specifically, no network outside of my Cisco colleagues, a friend and I formed a monthly Thursday happy hour for headquarter locals. Over the next two years, the happy hours got nicknamed "Black Thursday" as they slowly turned into goodbye parties. One by one, our happy hour crew left Cisco, but stayed in touch at these monthly gatherings, gradually creating an intra-company network. It was cheating a little bit because I worked with these people for so long, but it worked.

How about mere acquaintances? When I moved to the Bay Area, I stretched my finances to the max to put my children in an international school. Growing up multilingual, it was important for me to give my children the gift of language and exposure to culture. Another mother, whose daughter instructed her to get to know the new mom with purple hair, spotted me in the parking lot and invited me to a back-to-school breakfast for third-grade parents. I accepted and, wow, was she impressive. Houda Rahim was one of those irritatingly put together people. She was an intelligent, kind, cultured, Stanford engineering graduate turned stay-at-home entrepreneur once she had children. One friend led to another, and I established a monthly Wednesday happy hour for enterprising mothers. These women loved their families, but they had much more to talk about than the husbands and diapers in their lives. It may be non-traditional, but who says men get to corner the market on developing their professional network over drinks?

Now I was getting the groove of things. With the friendlies, it was easy to be curious about their stories. As an introvert that has learned to access my ambivert, I needed to push myself a little further with total strangers. I brought the same genuine curiosity I had with my friends to new interactions. In an audience, my inner nerd would raise a hand and ask the speaker a thought-provoking question. One on one, I can always find something genuinely intriguing about somebody that connects me to them. "I read a blog that you wrote," or "I agree/disagree with the question you asked," or "amazing shoes." Male or female, it's always about the shoes. Every authentic curiosity opened up a story, and I no longer found myself networking. I was creating meaningful connections.

Networking has gotten a bad reputation because it has been frightfully abused. We've all been to events where people walk up to you, extend their hand for a firm shake, and essentially say, "Hi, my name is Hang. What can you do for me?" Before you even give them your title, they launch into their elevator pitch. The next time someone does that to you, try interrupting them in the middle of it. They're so rehearsed, they likely would have forgotten their own name. As they're shaking your hand to bid you farewell, they're already looking past you at the next person who might be more interesting. Sound familiar? Yeah—don't do that. While you may think people can't see right through the act, they are absolutely internally crossing you off their list of care-abouts. Intention matters.

By the time I left corporate to start my company, interesting leads came in from random parts of my network that I didn't expect. A happy hour colleague here. A cool international school mom there. A random connection from one of my networking events. A friend of a client. A client of a friend. Although I took a big risk to forego my salary and benefits, it was incredibly rewarding and a little bit astonishing to be able to replace my corporate salary within 18 months.

New You, New Role

What if you want to use your newly found brand and networking skills for a new corporate job? When you're ready to move on, make an exit plan. Help your network help you. If you don't know what you want, neither will your network or prospective boss. There's a difference between refusing to settle and requiring impossible criteria. I've spent countless hours acting as a career therapist provoking the following introspection.

Categorize your priorities into "Must Haves" and "Nice to Haves." Then pick the Top 3.

- Corporate Culture
- Challenge / Opportunity to Learn
- Impact
- Title / Opportunity for Advancement
- Salary
- Industry / Functional Organization Change
- Temporal Flexibility / Proximity to Home

Besides being very fortunate, very creative, or both, you cannot expect to make a career change in a new industry at a higher title and salary than you left, that allows you to work 20 hours per week within five minutes from home. Not gonna happen. Get over it.

Clearly articulate your value. Now is your time to get out of any pigeonhole roles that leverage your talent, but not your passion. What do you want to do, and how you are going to do it? Vague answers like, "I've done everything," and "I can do anything" may be true, but they leave your advocates wondering, "huh?". It's not easy, and it takes work to determine what you want to be when you grow up.

Now, get out there. You've already done the hard work above. No one's going to know who you are unless you put yourself out there, in person and online. Get over your social media allergies, and meet your audience where they engage, online. My friend and author of *Digital-First Leadership*, Richard Bliss says, "The inability to master 21st century communication tools calls into question your ability to lead a 21st century organization."

- *LinkedIn*: Update your profile with a professional photo, maximize every character in your headline, and be thoughtful in writing your "about" section. That two-minute pitch should come in handy here. Give it some authentic professional motivation, philosophy, and passion. It is not a platform for a boring copy-paste of your resume.
- *Resumes*: Don't simply ask a colleague to help you. Actually do the work of viewing their company website, finding open job requisitions, and tailoring your CV for that role. Ask them if there are specific roles coming up that may not be listed. Make it easy on your network.

Catalytic Choices

Opportunities can arise out of challenging moments if you have the ability to recognize three components:

1. A *forcing function* that pushes you out of your comfort zone
2. A *catalytic connection* who is willing to stake their reputation on an endorsement for you
3. A *risk-taker* to gamble on your potential expertise

Let's retrace some of my history to see if it follows the model.

Joining Cisco

- *Forcing function*: I wanted to go into marketing, and my only opportunity was to move to California
- *Catalytic connection*: My ex-husband's director introduced me to Cisco marketing
- *Risk-taker*: The product line manager who took me on without marketing experience

Becoming an entrepreneur

- *Forcing function*: Layoff #3 and subsequent health crisis
- *Catalytic connections*: My network from various corners
- *Risk-takers*: The clients who took a gamble out of respect for their friend or colleague

Going Back to Corporate

As a consultant, one of my biggest clients was a cybersecurity company that was striving to triple its revenue. One of my ex-Cisco Black Thursday colleagues introduced me to the field marketing team at Gigamon. Eighteen months into my contract, a requisition in sales enablement came up. I called the hiring manager to share my perspective. Having been in that role for a much larger company, I asked Brad Shafer, Head of Sales Engineering, about his goals and the critical part that new role might be to the company's revenue goals. My point of view was the position could drive much more impact if the scope was broadened to be more strategic versus execution oriented.

He answered flatly, "I'm already pretty much at offer with someone else," to which I answered that I was quite happy as a consultant at this juncture and didn't intend to go back to corporate. I just wanted to offer a collaborative conversation as someone vested in my client's success and deeply engaged in the transformation of that field. As a bonus, I wasn't even charging him for the consultation! By the time we were done, he asked if I'd like to interview for the job, to which I answered, "Not the way it's currently written." It wasn't easy, but he was impressed enough that he up-leveled the requisition.

With residual corporate post-traumatic stress disorder, I still wasn't sure about putting a badge back on. On the last night of a tradeshow week, I read out our statistical outcomes to the crowd at dinner and asked the CEO to say a few words. He stood up to thank everyone and proceeded to instruct the room to spend the next two hours convincing me to take an offer he just approved for me that same day. How do you say no to that?

Professor Shafer now teaches at Northeastern Illinois University and occasionally asks me to guest lecture on entrepreneurship. At this point in the story, I'll pause as he reflects to his students, "She had a fearlessness that she brought with credibility. She painted a vision that opened me up to thinking differently about the role, and I began to reimagine the possibilities. We took enablement to a whole different level with amazing results in a company that didn't even know it needed it."

- *Forcing function*: A serendipitous job opening
- *Catalytic connection*: My friend from the Black Thursday crew
- *Risk-taker*: The head of sales engineering, who already filled the role before I came along

Becoming an Executive

Having learned my lessons from before, I continued to develop my expertise and curate my brand in person and online. I was confident in *what* I knew. I was building my network of *who* I knew. In order to become my own hero and pave my own path, I needed to establish a really solid foundation of credibility so the *people* I knew, knew *what* I knew. You can only blaze trails once you have a platform for your voice. Screaming without a platform is just creating noise. I began attending meetings with the Bay Area Marketing Association and the Sales Enablement Society. As it occurred with the international school in San Diego and women's networking groups in the Bay Area, the thoughtful questions I asked got me noticed. Soon, there would be a tap on the shoulder by the leaders of the organizations to become a leader within their organizations. One introduction would lead to another introduction, which would lead to another opportunity.

An enablement leader at another cybersecurity company hosted a group of leaders to share best practices. A few weeks later, a recruiter from an enterprise cloud communication company, called 8x8, contacted me. They were interested in my new cybersecurity friend, but the job wasn't a match for him. However, the discussion we had at his office left such an impression on him that he strongly recommended the recruiter reach out to me, someone he barely knew. My digital footprint from the various articles I had written, my speaking sessions, and overall social media engagement gave the hiring executive, Scott Sampson, SVP of Enterprise Sales, a sense of my thought leadership before I stepped into the room. I was offered my first executive role by a sales leader who truly saw me for all my potential and challenged me to bring my best game. As I was leaving 8x8, the most impressive enterprise sales leader I had worked with told me, "You're the best natural hire I've made in my career."

I was only there for six months when I received a message on Linked-In. Bing.

Hey Hang! Lots of changes at Juniper these days. I'm pumped about what we're doing. Our new Chief Customer Officer mentioned to me that he'd like to bring on board a sales enablement leader. Your name immediately came to mind. Thanks! Rami

I had met the man three or four times before. The first time, my friend, Houda, introduced me to her husband, Rami, at a Halloween gathering. He said, "I see you have a Cisco water bottle. I'm with Juniper." I did *not* put two and two together. After a little bit of mutual harassment, we proceeded to discuss the practicality of sending children to a multilingual school. Will they fall behind in English? Will they forget French anyway as they grow up? I threw down all my international school board member statistics and passion. When I left that night, he asked, "What do you do?"

I didn't see him again until two years later at his daughter's birthday party. Enough time had passed that I had gotten a little savvier. This time, I walked up to him and said, "I have a bone to pick with you. You aren't *with* Juniper, you *are* Juniper." The CEO chuckled at me and proceeded to talk about the state of technology. As we left the trampoline gym, he departed with, "Remind me again, what do you do?" I'm not going to make the man ask me a third time. My curiosity intrigued him. I connected with him on LinkedIn and occasionally interacted with posts from him or his team. His feed would occasionally surface my content, reminding him of what I do and how I think about what I do.

A couple years after that? Bing. Is this for real? How do you say no to that? Most people without access don't have friends who are wives of CEOs. You can create your own access with intention, work, and some sacrifice, while maintaining your authenticity. As I mentioned, I scrimped every penny to move to the Bay Area, where I would move six times in six years as a single mother. I spent every extra minute I could to create these networks. Even when access is provided, it doesn't guarantee success. I still had to *earn it and own it*. My interview panel consisted of half the e-suite and several sales leaders. Terrifying. Who knew that embracing my edge by rocking purple hair in a schoolyard parking lot would lead to the biggest job I've had to date? Be a good human. To everybody.

- *Forcing function*: A serendipitous job opening
- *Catalytic connection*: A third-grade kid and her very impressive mother
- *Risk-taker*: The CEO and head of sales

In all of these situations, I learned to take the "ick" factor of "working my net" out of networking. I learned to put myself out there by making genuine connections and collaborating authentically, without expectations of favors in return. It's disarming, and it makes a lasting impact. In any of these situations, I could have hesitated to seize the opportunity, but the window would have closed. One of my favorite sayings is by stoic philosopher, Seneca the Younger, "Luck is when opportunity meets preparation." I had been preparing. For years. Without access, I needed to put myself on the radar. When finally given the chance, I was more than ready to own my seat at the table. I was ready to embrace the *Girl on Fire* in Alicia Keys' song.

Chapter 12
Melting the Glass Ceiling

"We knew we did not lay down the direction for the street, but despite that, we could—and must—fashion the way of our walk."
– From *Between the World and Me*, by Ta-Nehisi Coates

Are you tired of the diversity conversation? It's understandable—it's been long, it's been hard, and it's exhausting. But unfortunately, it has to get worse before it gets better. The conversation needs to continue until equality is no longer breaking news. We need to open those uncomfortably honest discussions between men, women, and people of all colors until inequality falls into the annals of history as an odd reflection. What? Families used to watch public lynchings as part of their Sunday stroll after church? Couples were thrown in jail for interracial marriage? How absurd does that sound today? Think of women's suffrage, desegregation, and the legality of gay marriage. When's the last time you heard a discussion in the United States about the validity of a woman's right to vote or a Thanksgiving conversation extolling the merits of separate bathrooms for separate races? I dream of a day when we don't have to talk about equal pay for equal work. I dream of a day when we have to replace a female justice on the highest court of the land with a male justice in order to create balance.

For that to happen, empathy has to come from both sides. We have to be able to speak *with* each other, rather than *at* each other, so we can collaborate on driving a solution. We need to hear the struggles of women whose careers have hit a moat of molasses beyond their control. We need to appreciate when majority populations take ownership of their privilege, and we need to acknowledge their feelings of reverse discrimination. To that end, neither victim blaming nor privilege shaming effectively brings along the voices of champions from the other side.

Before we demonize white men, let's remember that Mildred Loving, a black woman in Virginia, was only able to keep herself and her white husband, Richard Loving, out of jail by writing a letter to a white man, Robert Kennedy. As a result, a 28-year-old white lawyer from the American Civil Liberties Union fought their case pro bono for years, ultimately landing the case in front of the United States Supreme Court, where 9 white men voted to declare anti-miscegenation, the romantic intermingling of people of different races, to be unconstitutional. Let's celebrate every person, whether in the majority or minority, who has a hand in advancing humanity.

My belief in the goodness of humanity trusts that, *in general*, unconscious bias exhibits without malicious intent. Martin Luther King famously said, "The arc of the moral universe is long, but it bends toward justice." I think of progressing equality as "melting," rather than "breaking" or "shattering," the glass ceiling. Because vocabulary matters. Intention matters. "Breaking" is a violent word that implies an "us" versus "them" model. What will be the collateral damage on either side? My journey in advocacy has taught me that people will only change when they're ready to listen, and they will only listen if we can speak in an empathetic language they can process. In today's contentious environment, we've forgotten how to leave space for dialogue. Artificial Intelligence and echo chambers feed us what we want to hear. The internet and social media have democratized access to voice, but it has also opened the gates to rage and manipulation. I have to believe that our evolved minds are better than our social media feeds and the loudest voices of division. When possible, I'm a proponent of evolution over revolution.

We acknowledged from the very beginning in calling out the good, the bad, and the ugly, that life isn't fair. There's no use in bemoaning, "I could be really successful *if* life was perfect." It's important to either find or form a community every time the sands shift so we can navigate within the reality that we live in and push boundaries with audacity. Doing this will require a village of mentors and sponsors to support us as individuals, as well as allies and role models to support the overall cause for equality.

Mentors advise you from a position of experience. Good advice comes in small bites from everyone around you. They can include, but are not limited to, people in your leadership. They can be your peers. They can be your employees. Some of my best mentors are the people who work for me. I often have one of the most diverse teams, including young talent. They're important for keeping us current and relevant. My kids tell me all the time how uncool I am and how much I don't know. It keeps me humble that as far as they're concerned, I'm never the smartest person in the room. I'm a freaking house plant that doesn't know what's up.

When interacting with a mentor, think about how they can help you work *through* a situation with their experience or area of expertise. Brainstorm with them where and how you might come up with different solution scenarios.

Sponsors advocate for you from a position of influence. While mentors may be able to provide sage wisdom when you're together, sponsors will amplify your personal brand, your professional reputation, when you're not in the room. In corporate, decisions about your career are made when you're not in the room. If you're an entrepreneur, decisions to retain your agency happen when you are not in the room. Certainly, your manager can be your sponsor, but you also need to develop advocates among other leaders with access and who carry influence with the main decision makers at the next level. It's your manager's job to either take care of you or manage you out. Sponsors don't have any obligation to you, so the weight of their support speaks volumes about your work ethic and performance. Sponsorship begets further sponsorship. These are the folks who will be critical in providing you the catalytic connections we talked about that will offer you catalytic choices.

When interacting with a sponsor, think about how they can help you work *to* a new situation. If you're trying to solve a problem, give them three options you've come up with, your recommendation, and get their perspective on the process you used to come to your conclusion. By giving them options, you show diligence. By giving them a recommendation, you show value. By explaining your process, you show thoughtfulness and the humility to ask for advice. What about the next steps for your success? Can your sponsor outline what the decision process might look like? Can they identify and maybe even connect you to the key decision makers?

Allies affect change with their leverage. Social transformations in history can only be realized when those in power speak out on behalf of an underrepresented class. In every social battle, we have to have partners from both sides. In each American movement, the abolition of slavery required an Abraham Lincoln to a Frederick Douglass. Women's suffrage could not have occurred without Max Eastman's partnership with Susan B. Anthony. The Civil Rights movements needed a John F. Kennedy to a Martin Luther King, Jr. In these three situations, the person in the majority (example: JFK) was not sponsoring the career of *the individual* in the minority (example: MLK). The person in the majority wielded their authority and influence in support of *the cause* represented by the person in the minority. One person was not subservient to the other; they were partners who needed each other. At work, it's important to know who your allies are in order to ensure you are in a non-toxic environment that nurtures everyone equally.

And finally, *role models* are people who share some aspect of your background that you can look up to. When you're looking at changing companies or organizations within a company, look at the inner circles. Every executive has one—is that circle of three to five people diverse enough? Does it include a woman or a person of color? Look at the executive ownership for diversity initiatives. I highly recommend to leaders that if they insist on having a white male owner, they need to at least have a co-owner who is a diverse role model. Sometimes the reason is that there isn't a woman in the organization with a high enough title. Then keep going down in titles until you find someone. If it's too far down, find someone from another organization. Representation matters.

No matter how well meaning and passionate that white man is, he has never walked in the shoes of those he is trying to advocate. A movement is most effective when an ally partners with a role model who can credibly tell the story of those who are impacted. JFK needed MLK to derive empathy for a human experience he could never fully understand. Both parts are equally important to moving *the cause* forward. The ally provides access to a platform for the role model to share their voice. Before you make a choice to join an organization, look to see if there are allies and role models around. Their absence may be a significant red flag.

As a woman, and especially as a minority, it is up to you to establish your community of access. White men of privilege have it built in. You can be upset that it's unfair, or you can do something about it and establish this network for yourself. Think about each role: can you instantly name some personal mentors and sponsors? If not, go find people within and outside of your organization who can amplify your reputation before you walk in the room. Can you instantly name two or three allies and role models who are fighting the good fight for the cause? If not, can you be the ally for a group more marginalized than your own, or a role model for those below you? Who's in your circle? Does it include a diverse mix of people?

With all of these roles, don't walk around asking, "Will you be my mommy? Will you be my mentor? Will you be my sponsor?" Please don't do that. This is where you really need to *earn it, own it, evolve it*. Kick ass at *what* you do and be extremely collaborative in *how* you do it. My prior boss, Scott Sampson, used to advise me all the time, "Bring people under the tent." Do good work. Document what you've done and who you've worked with to make sure you've been inclusive enough to have everyone's fingerprint on the program.

Then put it out there in such a way that people want to work with you. You can self-advocate without self-accolading. Remember, I'm highly sensitive to the "ick" factor of inauthentic self-promotion, whether it's in person, over email, or on social media. There is a subtle, but important, difference between sharing the problems your team has solved in service of a corporate or customer outcome versus reporting what you've done. For instance, my team doesn't deliver training. They ensure that our sales force stays current in knowledge, that our processes maximize efficiency, and that we continuously maintain a modern approach to sales. We don't report what we do; we report our outcomes. Success is no longer about access to information or execution of singular activities. Success is about who can make sense of vast amounts of data, pinpoint problems, and develop creative solutions.

If you want to be noticed, be noticeable. Effectiveness is the intersection of your relentless relevance in your field and impeccable situational analysis. Add a sprinkle of authentic personality and boom! Mentors and sponsors are going to want to be a part of your journey. They're going to want to be known for spotting your spark and helping to polish that diamond in the rough.

The journey doesn't end when you get an invitation to the room. Representation in the room does not ensure a voice at the table. What's your role? Be clear or get clear. Are you serving, are you sitting, or are you speaking? Get an understanding from your mentors, sponsors, allies, and role models so you can prepare accordingly. Once you get there, do the best you can to melt the glass ceiling for others behind you.

Collectively Disrupt the Myths

Let's talk about what women have been told they need to fix, an implication that they are somehow already broken. A side effect of the recent rise of the quest for gender equality is a disproportionate volume of well-meaning instructions that are specifically geared toward women only. Leadership training for women has often focused on making us more like men. In 2005, social scientists Rosalind Barnett and Caryl Rivers described the divide between the sexes as a crevice, not a chasm, in the book, *Same Difference: How Gender Myths are Hurting Our Relationships.*

On confidence. Women are often coached to make more of an effort to sit at the table and raise their hands and voices. When I lead diversity workshops, I make it a point to invite men into the conversation. When there are 50 women and a handful of men, guess who the quiet ones are sitting in the back of the room? When the few men do speak up, guess who is now in the majority, minimizing the men's voices, as we so often experience ourselves. Witnessing these behaviors, I don't believe that it's a matter of women being naturally more docile and men being intentional bullies.

When someone is in the majority, it's easier to have their voice heard. When someone is in the minority, they're not necessarily more timid; they're just more judicious about when to speak up and more thoughtful about when to speak out. Quiet observation is simply smart survival. It makes it that much more important to call on the minority in the room to share their opinion, because they're actually listening, instead of waiting to talk. In a room full of men, call on a woman. In a room full of women, call on a man. In a white audience, call on the minority; in a room full of minorities, call on the white person—not because you're catering to anyone, but because they have been the most observant and least susceptible to groupthink. How interesting would their perspective be?

On demeanor. Women get much more specific advice to walk a certain way, talk a certain way, dress a certain way, pointing to a *qualitatively* stricter set of requirements for women to achieve business acceptance. These are the struggles of ambitious women, the tightrope we walk, and the longer yardstick by which we are measured. We have to excel so much more just to be even. My favorite guidance? Powerful people take up a lot of space. Spread out your body and spread out your stuff. At the same time, women are criticized for coming into meeting rooms two minutes late with a bunch of crap, looking disorganized. So, am I supposed to bring stuff to spread out or not? I am a petite 5'3" woman who wields only a notebook and is fond of wearing skirts. I will continue to travel light and cross my legs, thank you very much.

On emotions. It is absolute crap when women are indicted for being emotional. Women often show their frustration with displays of vulnerability (yes, this includes tears). Men often show their frustration by increasing their dominance (this includes increased volume and shorter tempers). Women often show their displeasure by withdrawal, while men tend to do the same with passive aggressiveness. Humans are all emotional beings, full stop. These are all emotional responses. Certain cultures display power with assertiveness, while others show power with quiet leadership. Do not mistake vulnerability as a sign of weakness.

Instead of having a conversation about women being emotional, let's think about it in terms of women's ability to hear the needs of each person in the room. I'm going to let you in on a secret. We have the ability to *accept* other people's feelings without *agreeing* to all their opinions. Chris Voss, former FBI hostage negotiator, brings it together nicely. When I asked him at the previously discussed Happy Hour, "How do you think men and women negotiate differently, and what are the best attributes of each?" His answer was,

> Men are stereotyped as being more assertive. Women are stereotyped to be emotional or relationship oriented. Both aspects are necessary elements. You've got to be assertive, just don't be a jerk about it. If you don't assert your own best interest, you're asking the other side to guess what's good for you. The

percentage conversion rate on guessing isn't high. So, you have to stand up for yourself without being a jerk. Being highly relationship conscious is a critical aspect to developing a great long-term relationship. There's a fine line between needing to be liked and being likable. If you're likable, you're six times more likely to make a deal. I want to be likable, but if I need to be liked, I've taken myself hostage. So, there are aspects to both that ultimately, whether you're a man or a woman, you learn about what makes the other side successful and you add it to your existing strengths.

- Chris Voss

On likeability. That's one point for women for leveraging their emotional awareness to further relationships. But we just hit the next pitfall—the ominous "L word" for women in positions of power. The "likability penalty" is a term coined by Sheryl Sandberg, Facebook's Chief Operating Officer and founder of the Lean In Foundation. The phrase reflects how women in business need to assert themselves in order to be viewed as effective. However, assertive women are viewed as aggressive and intimidating, words that are rarely used to describe assertive men.

A 2007 report from the Catalyst Group, *Damned if You Do, Doomed if You Don't*, reveals the "double-bind dilemma." "Women leaders are perceived as competent *or* liked, but rarely both." It's time to challenge the gender association to likeability. If we see it, we should call it out. If negative words are used to describe confident women, we should use the Contrast Principle to set context in relative versus absolute terms. Simply ask, "Compared to what or to whom? To John?" Sallie Krawcheck, CEO and co-founder of Ellevest Network, has written that we should redefine "likable" to center on ability and honesty. And "if a woman we don't personally like happens to succeed ... we need to celebrate the victory."

On wardrobe. It's impossible to win a game where the rules are constantly changing around you, and judgement is random. In one of my workshops, I share a story about how hurt I was when a "friend" showed me a text from another "friend" about how inappropriately dressed I was at a cocktail gathering. My "friend" didn't relay this information from a place of kindness. It was coming from a place of judgement and their own urge to give unsolicited advice.

I asked the audience, "What do you think I was wearing? What if I told you it was a black blouse, black pants, black pumps, and a black blazer. What if I told you it's the exact same outfit I'm wearing today?" The women and men were all caught by surprise. They hadn't noticed anything unusual about my outfit all day. How could something this innocuous fall to such harsh judgement?

Because the blouse was sleeveless. For shame! And the outfit was form fitting. Heaven forbid! What does this have to do with skill, will, and effectiveness? When Michelle Obama emerged as the first lady, there was a controversy called "Sleevegate" around her wardrobe. While multiple first ladies, including Jackie Kennedy, wore their sleeveless tops with fashion, Michelle Obama wore her sleevelessness with power. Despite all the drama, she continued to do so. Channel your inner Katniss Everdeen from the *Hunger Games*. If you're going to do all the work and still be invisible, go ahead and shoot that arrow through the apple in the pig's mouth. Sisters, set your arms free! If I was going to be penalized for non-conformance, I might as well go big. That week, I colored my hair purple, as well. For the many of us who are already kicking ass, the challenge is finding a supportive environment to thrive. Or we can make our own.

If we acknowledge the existence of unconscious bias, in any small measure, don't we owe it to our daughters and sisters to break down these barriers? Today, I call on you to embrace your edge. You are perfect in your imperfection. Strive for better, not perfect, as you define it in your career and modern family. You ARE a fully capable woman. You may even have the additional perspective of being a minority woman. How boring to try to fit in as part of the majority. There is no need to think or act like a man. Think and act like a woman—bring ALL of your cognitive diversity to the table. As Oscar Wilde once said, "Be yourself; everyone else is taken." You do you.

Reflect on your own unconscious biases. We all have them—even those of us who promote equality. We are fighting generations of socialization. Remember the story about the girls on the playground? Who did you envision circling me? What if I told you it was three white girls and four minority girls from two groups who didn't play with each other, but decided to ban together this one time to gang up on me? What unconscious bias does this speak to within you?

Recalibrate. It's understandable to have these biases, but once you recognize it, it is your responsibility to choose how to act on it and lead by example. Those girls later became my friends, and more importantly, they became friends with each other through me, and they remained friends after I left.

Reset. Don't be afraid of who you are: intuitive, collaborative, and tenacious. Those are the gifts of your adversity. Don't worry about becoming fierce—as a professional woman, you already are.

Women are finally being celebrated for all their dimensions. Just as men can be competent engineers in flip flops and t-shirts, women can be competent professionals whether they choose to dress similarly or in high heels and skirts. It makes us no less intelligent, no less relevant, and no less impactful. In fact, women possess all the attributes critical for negotiation and influence: collaboration, listening, and empathy.

Immigrants and minorities are finally being celebrated for their resilience and resourcefulness. For immigrants, survival depends on the ability to move seamlessly between different environments: physically, emotionally, intellectually. Our adversity makes us scrappy and agile. As famously punctuated in the musical, *Hamilton*, "Immigrants, we get the job done."

A Reflection on Women in the Workplace

Let's reflect back on the graph at the beginning of the book. Another way to look at it is at the beginning, 64% of the professional population is white, increasing to 85% among executives. That share of population increases by 21%, whereas people of color drop from 36% to 15%, a massive decrease by 71%. In inclusion and diversity, we need to talk about two measurements: the size of the pie and the size of the slice. We don't like talking about the truth that the slices of the pie have to add up to 100%. In that respect, it is indeed a zero-sum game.

For minorities to reclaim their fair share, majorities are rightfully concerned about losing the size of their slice. But remember, I don't want any of *your* pie. I just want *my* piece of the pie. Why do you want my slice? That said, the conversation we miss is that when we bring diversity to the table, we are better together, and the size of the whole pie increases. In this respect, it is NOT a zero-sum game. Giving me more share of voice increases my pie slice, *as well as* yours! So, the net is more, for *all* of us. In this way, no one is protecting something that wasn't theirs to begin with. We change the conversation from what minorities want to *take*, and focus instead on what minorities can *make*, together.

I will ask the same question I posed in the beginning of the book again, "Do we really believe the shape of these various pipelines is a direct correlation to a lack of ambition or capability in women and people of color?" You've heard my story now. "Unintelligent. Lazy. Socially awkward." These are not words that people would use to describe me. Yet I was laid off three times and marginalized for much longer.

As a minority woman, there are times you are made to feel like the reason you are in a certain position is because of a need for tokenism. Remember to respond to that microaggression from an indisputable Adult state. "I'm not sure how it feels to get a job just because I'm a minority and/or woman, but I'm sure it feels a lot better than when I *didn't* get considered because of it." Don't let anyone diminish your accomplishment by implying that it's charity. The number of times it's worked against you likely far outnumbers the number of times it has worked for you. As Taylor Swift sings, "Haters gonna hate, hate, hate, hate ... ." Mean people suck. The best revenge is knowing your worth and succeeding, anyway. Shake it off. Take the win. It doesn't matter what people think about how you got there, just keep earning your place once you've arrived. You got to where you are *despite* your disadvantage, not *because* of it. Claim your piece of the pie and savor every warm bite. You deserve your desserts.

I could have easily fallen into the category of women who "opted out" of industry. But the irony is that I never quit working. Even with the birth of each child, I only took the requisite six weeks off, and I was itching to come back before my time was up. I left corporate because it was simply easier to create my own business where I can pick my clients, succeed unconstrained, and—deep breath—be valued and compensated for my performance. I came back to corporate on my own terms and to make a difference for women in the workplace behind me. As Lady Gaga wrote, I needed more in this modern world, so I ventured "far from the shallow."

The Paradoxical Commandments

In the back of my notebook, I've transcribed one of my favorite poems from the end of the documentary, *Bombshell,* about Hedy Lamarr, actress, inventor, and big thinker.

People are illogical, unreasonable, and self-centered.
Love them anyway.

If you do good, people will accuse you of selfish ulterior motives.
Do good anyway.

If you are successful, you will win false friends and true enemies.
Succeed anyway.

The good you do today will be forgotten tomorrow.
Do good anyway.

Honesty and frankness make you vulnerable.
Be honest and frank anyway.

The biggest men and women with the biggest ideas can be shot down by the smallest men and women with the smallest minds.
Think big anyway.

People favor underdogs but follow only top dogs.
Fight for a few underdogs anyway.

What you spend years building may be destroyed overnight.
Build anyway.

Give the world the best you have, and you'll get kicked in the teeth.
Give the world the best you have anyway.

– Kent M. Keith

Chapter 13
Pave It Forward

"... you may be the first to do many things—
make sure you're not the last."
– Shyamala Gopalan Harris, mother of the first female
US Vice President of color

What would have happened to me if my family had not run into the benefactors (the Officer, the Angel, and the Cook) who helped our escape from Vietnam? What if I wasn't caught by one chubby little hand by someone who had already made it onto the boat?

Character has been defined by Malcolm Forbes as how we treat someone we have the ability to mistreat, those in the shadows who we deem can do nothing for us or to us—the waiter, the cleaning staff, who have much to lose at a cranky customer's whim. My corollary is "character is defined by taking care of those we are not obligated to take care of."

At the end of the war, Operation New Arrivals relocated 130,000 Vietnamese refugees and prepared them for resettlement in the United States with the assistance of charitable civilian agencies. The foster family program was vital in teaching refugees how to strap their own boots. From

Fort Chaffee, Arkansas, we were flown to Chicago to meet our Lithuanian sponsor family. Having been immigrants themselves, Mr. and Mrs. Vytas and Briute Zalatorious paid it forward by helping us get acclimated to life in the United States. They provided guidance on simple things many of us take for granted, like how grocery stores worked in America versus the farmers markets with which we were accustomed. They brought us to the local Salvation Army to spend the little money we had to buy clothes we needed for school and work. When my sister visits the Zalatorious' home, she gazes at a large picture displayed in the middle of their living room of my family when we first arrived. Stuffed into the edges of the frame are little pictures each of us have sent them over the years of benchmark moments: graduations, marriages, and babies.

Once we were in Baton Rouge, my father's journey led him on a path to provide social impact for global citizens. He helped families who escaped the terror of oppression and abject poverty from all around the world. This exposure to living history early in my life has continued to shape my perspective on acceptance of all cultures, as I continuously challenge others to become more adaptable. Let's stop pretending that we can fully understand the experiences of others who come from vastly different backgrounds. Instead, let's focus on simple acknowledgement that we are different, with empathy for our individual perspectives of shared stories. Let's jointly resolve to melt the barriers of judgement from which we see each other. Reasonable conversations must take place between diverse individuals to authentically defeat bias in and outside of the workplace. I am hopeful for a day when concerns for my daughter's professional development is not so much more overwhelming than concerns for my son's development because of the many more obstacles she would face as a woman.

We are at a moment in history when there is tremendous momentum for change on the heels of the Women's March, the #metoo movement, and the election of a President who is brave enough to invite a qualified woman of color as his Vice-Presidential partner. I recall being on a panel with a C-level executive, who remarked on how much progress has been made since she began. She relayed a story about the coaching she received on her first day at work, fresh out of university. She was advised not to wear patterned dresses so as not to clash with the furniture in the office. Yes, we have come very far from that, but there is still so much further to go.

For too long, women and immigrants have been deprived of access: without information, choice, and voice. Our digital world has now democratized access to information, proliferated our opportunities, and social media has provided a meaningful platform for expression. Now is our time. My hope is that we acknowledge our own privilege, as well as the harder road for those without access. We need to stop blaming women and immigrants for their own plight. It would be like blaming a diligent worker for burning out because they handle more than their fair share of work, or blaming women for being so attractive that they're asking to be assaulted. Just because you *can* mistreat someone, doesn't mean you *should*. The act of telling someone you're going to take advantage of them, doesn't give you permission to do so.

At the beginning of our journey together, I promised to share raw stories from the trenches, laced with harsh disappointments and learnings that would lead to triumphs over challenges. Throughout this book, I talked about defining where you want to go and how to get there, better, not bitter. By using the three R's of reassessment and calibrating your three S's of success, my hope is that women who have been unseen, and minorities who have been unheard, feel empowered to celebrate their unique identity. I hope to have given you a framework to pave your own **CLEAR** path.

- Clarity: Be clear or get clear. Identify your values and define your purpose.
- Learn: *Earn it. Own it. Evolve it.* Become relentlessly relevant in your area of expertise. Learn from "received wisdom," as well as from your own experiments. That combined experience is what you uniquely bring to the table.

- **Edge:** Embrace the qualities derived from your unique experience—tenacity that has been shaped by adversity, the grit that comes from pain, the resourcefulness that comes from a lack of access, and the gratitude that comes from scarcity. Bring it all with you. Take agency *of* your disadvantage *for* your advantage.
- **Access:** Curate your own community. You don't have to be born with one to form one.
- **Responsibility:** Take accountability for what you can control while you're ascending. Once you get to each vista, pave the path for those behind you. Make it better, not harder for them.

It is important for us to share our stories. We have to prepare each other for the reality that life will be more unfair for us. But it is possible to rise above bad situations and make our own opportunities. We have to share our triumphs, so we have social proof that with work and tenacity, it is possible to climb out of the quagmire.

Once we get to the table, it is important to use our newfound access to initiate courageous conversations. And when we do, we should think about bestselling author, Daniel Pink's framework for influencing action.

1. What do you want them to know?
2. What do you want them to feel?
3. What do you want them to do?

A man asked me why women are so uncomfortable at work, when working with men is just an accepted norm. In response, I asked him, "What is the most uncomfortable situation you can imagine yourself in?" He said, "Miami nightclub." And I told him, "That's my life in corporate every damn day. And it's exhausting. Just because I can do it, doesn't make it right." I needed him to *know* how I feel, and *feel* how I feel. Phrasing my experience in his language created that lightbulb moment. As with any bad behavior, to defeat unconscious bias, we have to call it out when we see it. This is especially true once we have a voice at the table to shift the mindset of fellow leaders.

When the protests about racial injustice were happening during the COVID pandemic, I shared in the collective anger. I had been bullied by ignoramuses of all colors when I was young. But I was equally embraced by teachers and friends of those same colors the rest of my young life. I mourned with all my black friends and peers, whose frustration I could not fathom. With my new seat at a table, it was now time to initiate courageous conversations to influence action.

For my part, I attended my boss' weekly virtual staff meeting. After his update, we each got a turn to provide our own status. It was 5:30 in the morning. My office was dark. I remember taking a breath, turning my camera on, and I began tearing up before I even started speaking.

I know that the worst thing a woman can do in her career is to cry in front of 16 male vice presidents, but I'm going to do it anyway because I trust in the caliber of your character. I want you to know that this week has been really difficult for me because I grew up in the Deep South. These people were all my friends: black kids were my friends, white kids were were also my friends. I feel compelled to bring this up because I would be complicit if I didn't. I don't pretend to know what it's like to be black in America. But I understand discrimination. I understand the loneliness of onlyness. I want you to know that just because I've gotten used to being the only woman in the room for most of my career and being the only woman of color as I rose through the ranks, doesn't mean I'm comfortable with it, and it doesn't make it right. It is the character of the leadership in this organization that gives me the comfort to speak openly to you. My ask of you is not to be sad, not to be mad, but to DO something. Have a conversation with your family. Have a conversation with your team. Read. Learn. Vote. As a peer and fellow human being, I am asking you to DO something.

Most of them reached out to me separately afterward to say, "I heard you," followed by what they were going to do. I apologized to my boss for taking his staff call on a tangent. And he responded with, "People with your drive, achievement, and compassion will make the world different. I will ensure everyone plays a part in making the world better and fairer, even if it's only a little. Your passion shows your strength, not weakness. We are humans first and businesspeople second." This is my leader. This is why I work where I work. As with credibility for an individual, culture is hard to establish, easy to lose, and harder yet to recover in an organization. It's important to find a culture of acknowledgement, acceptance, and even appreciation in order to solve for the leaky pipeline of women and minorities in the workplace.

Embrace Your Edge

It's time for immigrant women to step into their courage and be vulnerable enough to embrace their whole true selves. We have to share the truth that the road is not full of sunshine and roses. It's not a simple, linear path of doing a good job and getting promoted into our aspiration. That's only the tip of the iceberg of ascension. I'm not even going to bother discussing the countless incidents of sexual misconduct by men or backstabbing by women. Let's start with calling out what's wrong and collaborate toward action. I had no idea how my message would be received in an executive forum with my boss and peers, or the repercussions I might be opening myself up to. It is scary to be bold, but the reward is high. Vote with your vote, vote with your dollar, vote with your voice.

My ask of you is to make a commitment to support each other, your peers, the youth to come, and the trailblazers before you. Stay engaged. Connect each other, be fierce advocates for each other, and stick up for each other when one person's voice is left unheard. Maximize your influence from above, below, and across the career lattice. Ask your peers to extend their friendship into mentorship of other women. Ask leaders to extend their mentorship into sponsorship and allyship.

Support the trailblazers so that they alone do not carry the burden of melting the glass ceiling for the rest of us to pass through. Don't mistake strength for indestructibility. After the initial glow from her book, *Lean In*, Sheryl Sandberg suffered a lot of criticism for her access. No story will 100 percent reflect our own. Sheryl started a great conversation among her male peers. She bravely brought up topics about motherhood, likeability, and the delicate navigation of the relationship between a male mentor/ sponsor with a female mentee/sponsee. Instead of attacking trailblazers for discrepancies to our own experience, let's give gratitude for the courage it took for them to lead the way, celebrate the progress they made, and continue to open even more conversations.

Women are moving away from the competitiveness that stems from the insecurity of fighting for that one seat at the table that might be available for us. We are working so much harder to give each other a hand up to claim our slices of the pie and make the pie bigger. It's been gratifying to watch this change. Come with me. Together, let's pull more chairs up to the table.

Part of my journey to fulfillment has been picking up others, but I had to be able to make that change in myself first. After 10 years of wanting to give up every day, my professional life began at the age of 45. It's never too late to manifest your dreams. I have known since I was 7 years old that I would write a book someday. Did I know when, how, and what topic? Absolutely not. From the moment I saw her video, I knew I would meet my idol, Carla Harris. She wrote to me a few weeks after I introduced her at our sales kick-off:

> As I board this flight in Dallas, my mind fell on you and your generosity. Continue to elevate and amplify your voice for my Spirit tells me that you have only begun. I wish you all the very best as you unapologetically step into your voice and your gift.
>
> – Warmly, Carla Harris

If this were a shirt she touched, I would never wash it.

Lessons are Taught, not Caught

When we talked about taking your expectations off road, I mentioned that I wanted to change the world. I wanted to show little girls what they could do, and I wanted to show little boys the endless possibilities of an equal partnership. Although I've always colored outside the lines, it's still scary to disobey the status quo. I question all the time if I am making the right choices. At the end of the day, I decided to love my children enough to expose my humanity to them. I could not live a 1950s life in 2010, and my hope is that I'm able to model authentic choices for them that will free them from living 1950s ideals in their own lives in 2050.

Second guessing. As with many working parents, I worry constantly about how my ambition affects how I show up at home. There has been overwhelming guilt of needing both a career and family, guilt that my children get less motherly time than their peers, guilt of enjoying travel for work but also as a break from caregiving. Beyond that, I wonder if I am fundamentally flawed in that I may not even be built that way. Even as a classroom parent when they were younger, it was never in my DNA to bake cookies for school or to hover over every homework assignment or test. All the kids in the classroom still knew who I was because I showed up on stage representing the board of trustees. I set high expectations and hope I've given my kids the motivation and tools to succeed. But with that point of view, am I paying enough attention to my children's educational, physical, and emotional needs? What deleterious effects will they suffer by being raised by a mom who has a need for achievement in her career? How much therapy are they going to need as adults?

On voice. With my experience of constantly being told to sit down and shut up, I have always encouraged my children to state their points of view ... and be prepared to defend them, if needed. I focused more on teaching them *how* to think, rather than exerting my will on *what* to think. I've always told them that my job is to give them the rules of life; their job is to figure out when to follow the rules and when not to. I told them initially I will win more arguments based on my life experience, but that over time I expect them to surpass me. And any day they can win me over to their point of view, would be a good day. They've had many good days.

On ambition. On one of my birthdays, my teenage son played a song for me on his guitar, and his younger sister gave me a small black canvas that she decorated in silver and gold. She handed me a marker and said, "Mommy, I want you to write the word 'fearless' on this, because that's what I think of you." I asked her to find a stencil so we can write it more beautifully, more perfectly. Her response, "You're missing the point—I know you're insecure about your handwriting, so I want you to keep being fearless." In that game-changing moment, I was overwhelmed with pride and relief. My children were giving me permission to keep being bold, to keep doing big things, and to keep being fierce.

I wanted to teach my children courage; they learned to be bold. A Money magazine article reports that "Children of working mothers tend to have more egalitarian views on gender roles. Their daughters are more likely to be financially independent with their own careers, and their sons tend to share more household chores." Whether parents work or not is neither right nor wrong—the importance is giving each other the choice to define our own destinies.

On marriage. My husband and I split up because we wanted to set each other free to be the best people we could be without each other. Right before my son left for college, my children and I stayed up one night baking a cake at 2 a.m. In a moment of guilt, I asked my kids about our little modern family.

Me: "Do you ever wish your parents stayed together?"
Son: "No, you wouldn't be happy."

Me: "What about if we were still married right now? Roman, you're about to leave for college. Bella, you're almost done with high school. Would you want us to wait to split up?"
Daughter: "No, you need to be happy every day you can."

Me: "But what if you didn't know?"
Daughter: "The kids always know. All the kids in high school know which parents should break up."

Me: "How do they know? I mean, like the family friends we spent the weekend with—could you tell? (We had not told any of the kids that the couple were about to file for divorce.)
Daughter: "Oh yeah, totally. I mean, not the first day, but definitely over the next two days."
Son: "You can just see the lack of closeness. Actually, I take it back. Sometimes the kids don't know, and it's because they've accepted sadness as normal."

I'm thinking, my son isn't quite the emotionally stunted teenager I thought he was, after all. Who is this guy? While I was still longing for a traditional family, my children learned to focus on content, not form.

On love. After the divorce, my hope was that if one or both of us were to re-couple, perhaps our children would grow up witnessing adults in very healthy and authentic relationships. Neither of us have re-partnered meaningfully, which means I often feel like a failure for not modeling two people in love for my children. Would it have been better to keep our family together, like most people? I was on speakerphone with one of my girlfriends who was excited about a new man she had just met.

Friend: "This guy is so incredible. He's so out of my league."
Me: "That's great, but what the hell is wrong with you? You're beautiful, you're smart, you're funny."

Friend: "Don't you ever worry about someone being out of your league?"
Me: I laughed, "Not anymore."
My daughter pops her head into the room: "Mommy IS the league."

I wanted to teach my children what a relationship between two people in love looks like. My children witnessed something else I didn't expect. They learned uncompromising self-worth.

On entitlement. As I mentioned, this book is *not* written for my children, who are part of the privileged class. They don't bathe in milk flown in from cows that roam free in the Australian outback, but they don't want for anything, either. They have food on the table, shoes on their feet, and a roof over their heads. They receive a fine education, exposure to arts, athletics, and travel. By far, the most important privilege they have is access to people and paths that are "off the menu." Raising them has given me a bird's-eye view into how much the path for privilege starts early and how easily privilege can slip into entitlement.

I often worry that being a working mom puts too much strain on my children. I was much more tiger mom than helicopter mom. Don't like your grade? Go talk to the teacher—I'm not doing it for you. Don't like your teacher? You're going to have bosses and peers you're not going to like. Figure it out. Think life is unfair? Yup, it is. No one helped me with my homework. My parents were busy putting food on the table, and my siblings were putting themselves through college by the time I got to middle school. Just as I turned to the library for help, my kids learned to be just as resourceful with the Internet to get it done while their mom was frantically rebuilding her life.

When my son turned 18, I turned over his entire college fund to him. "I won't be around forever; it's yours to use or lose." When he needed to transfer his finances, I gave him phone numbers to call. When he needed a record of his immunizations, I handed him his insurance card and told him to figure it out. A short three weeks after he started college, my son came home to attend my brother's 60th birthday. He told me how stressed he was having to figure out everything on his own. In contrast, he was surprised how dependent his fellow freshmen still were on their parents to manage logistics of daily life. I asked him what he thought the difference was, to which he answered, "I think good training to be independent, and my own ability to adapt."

I had hoped to teach my children independence; they learned to be self-sufficient.

On role models. My nieces are in their 20s now. One of them called to tell me that the experiences I warned her about were happening to her right now, and she was so glad to have honest guidance on how to navigate through it. One of my nephews came to visit after a tour with the Marines. My brother and I were having a heated conversation over dinner. My brother was telling Roman how important it was that he studies hard and gets a good job so he can take care of his woman and family. That makes the hair on the back of my neck stand up. I replied that partners should *choose* to need each other out of mutual admiration and not out of obligation. As the conversation escalated, my nephew turned to my kids and said, "Do you know how lucky you are?" He raised a glass of whiskey to me, and said, "All I gotta say is, successful women are attractive." Can I get a, "Hell, yeah!"

These are the lessons from the next generation. Every generation before tends to belittle the generation after, but just because they're different doesn't mean they're wrong. The world will continue to change, and normal will never return to yesterday. If we dismiss the younger generations, we're missing out on a competitive advantage of peeking into the crystal ball of what will be relevant in the future. What we view as the next generation's entitlement has given them permission to challenge the status quo. They value balance over affluence; they value sustainability over stuff. They have redefined success, including loving and equal partnerships.

This is why my team is also rich in diversity in age and tenure. One end brings wisdom; the other brings untapped potential. In all cases, I hire for capability, passion, and hunger. Fearlessness does not only require courage, it requires the freedom to make choices. Freedom from traditional expectations of primary provider versus primary caregiver. Freedom from well-intended, but misguided overprotectiveness. We must give women the choice to follow their limitless potential and trust in their capability to find their own professional and personal balance.

Former President Barack Obama wrote in his book, *A Promised Land*, "... our challenges are daunting. If I remain hopeful about the future, it's in large part because I've learned to place my faith in my fellow citizens, especially those of the next generation... ."

Conclusion

We have to share our stories so that women, minorities, and immigrants are celebrated for their talent, drive, and refreshing perspective. Just knowing that you are not alone matters. Everyone goes through stuff, and yet, regardless if the clouds impede your view, the sun rises every morning.

These days, my mornings are all very similar. My internal clock wakes me as the darkness gives way to dawn, casting a light blue hue on everything in the room. After making myself a cup of tea, I sit on the living room couch to listen to NPR's summary of world news. I watch the sky transition to purple and pink as daylight peeks over the hills of northern California. The beauty in these moments allows me to reflect with gratitude on how far my siblings and I have come from penniless immigrants to established professionals. The news keeps me grounded in how far the world has come and how much runway each of us has to reach our potential. Every morning, I feel an immense responsibility to share my story to encourage others to share *their* stories. We are all individually unique and collectively complete. Only if we can give ourselves the space to listen can we give our minds the ability to learn.

As I mentioned at the beginning, I can't define your endgame for you. This will be as far as I can take you. It will be up to you to take the first step with courage and to continue along your path with clarity. What actions will you take? What opportunities will you make? What will be the lessons that you pass down? As the Highwomen sing, "I want a house with a *Crowded Table*."

Acknowledgements

The guiding lights in my life have been my children, Roman and Isabella Black, who have supported me in my purpose. My children and my 17 nieces and nephews inspire me to hopefully leave the world a little better than we found it, for the generations behind us. No matter the time or distance, I am thinking of you always: Harrison Duong, Hyatt Duong, Hans Duong, Winston Tran, Danielle Tran, Eileen Huynh, Travis Huynh, Christine Huynh, Courtney Tran, Ryan Tran, Elizabeth Nguyen, Tiffany Nguyen, Tiffany Tran, Jessica Tran, Alyssa Tran, Brittany Brown, and Brianna Brown. I'd like to give a special call out to my mini-me, birthday twinsie, and ex-housemate, Tiffany. You have turned out to be every inch as deliberate, clever, and delightfully mischievous as the seven-month-old I first met. The sassy girl has grown wonderfully into a badass woman.

The story may not have ever been a story without the courage of my parents, Hue Tran and Huu Luu, and the tenacity to survive of my seven Tran siblings, Duyen, Dat, Hoang, Phuc, Phuong, Duc, and Anh. After my parents' passing, I have especially counted on my oldest sister, Duyen, to take their place in her loving acceptance of me.

And of course, I would not have been able to take on this endeavor without the continued partnership in caretaking for our children from my ex-husband, Bob Black.

The road has been long and unexpected with sponsors and supporters along the way: Joe Lebowitz from my days at Advanced Micro Devices, and the risk taker in my first career fork in the road, James Collinge. Throughout my years at Cisco, I have to thank Suraj Shetty and Kelly Ahuja for their continuous sponsorship. After Cisco, I thank the risk-takers who believed in my capability: John McCormack, James Werner, Brad Shafer, Scott Sampson, and Rami Rahim. In this latest adventure, I thank Marcus Jewell for being the first sponsor I have had in my career, who has consistently pushed me to reach my potential and pushed others to give me the opportunity to do so.

Then there are my closest confidantes who kept the light of inspiration ignited and extracted the deepest introspection from me, Scott Sampson, Linn Bekins, and Janet Bell. Finally, there is the #HangWithHang book club, who have listened to me read, write, whine, write, and read again, chapter after chapter. For the longest time, I hated working with women, until I eventually figured out that I was just working with the wrong women. To this special group of sisters, thank you for helping change my mindset about how we honor each other without judgement: Houda Rahim, Alla Oks, Bindu Garapaty, Marcela Rodriguez, Jennifer Tsang Hirsch, Andrea Vanegas, Naomi Elia, Jessica Garrison, Kia Cottrell, Stephanie White, Ashley Fordham, Lauren Malhoit, Tania Craythorne, Kala Jarugumilli, Irene Zhang, Row Heydarian and Surbhi Kaul.

May all your voices be as big as your hearts.

About The Author

A Vietnamese immigrant, dedicated mother, and seasoned technology executive, Hang Black has an extensive background in engineering, marketing, sales leadership, and entrepreneurship.

Hang is a global speaker on sales, leadership, and diversity and inclusion in the workplace. She holds a BS in Chemical Engineering from the University of Texas at Austin and lives in Los Altos, California with her two children.

"My hope is that women who have been unseen, and minorities who have been unheard, feel empowered to celebrate their unique identity."